D0088591

star*parenting

Sherrynne Dalby

star parenting

What astrology reveals about your
child's personality and potential

inspired
LIVING

ALLEN&UNWIN

The information in this book is intended as a guide only, and should not substitute medical care or advice. Always consult your doctor about supplements, dietary requirements and general medical advice in the first instance.

First published in 2009

Inspired Living, an imprint of
Allen & Unwin
83 Alexander Street
Crows Nest NSW 2065
Australia
Phone: (61 2) 8425 0100
Fax: (61 2) 9906 2218
Email: info@allenandunwin.com
Web: www.allenandunwin.com

Cataloguing-in-Publication details are available
from the National Library of Australia
www.librariesaustralia.nla.gov.au

ISBN 978 1 74175 766 8

Internal design by fisheye design, Sydney
Set in 10.5/14 pt Goudy Oldstyle by Bookhouse, Sydney
Printed in Australia by McPherson's Printing Group

10 9 8 7 6 5 4 3 2 1

To parents and children everywhere—and particularly to my own: Samantha, Nicole, Cassandra, Jarrad, Caitlin, Liam and Thomas.

contents

Foreword

Star Parenting **offers** a uniquely deep understanding of your child and outlines the various stages along the way to unlocking their potential, step by step.

The explanation of each planet's connection to your child's personality shows how these planets influence each of the developmental stages of childhood and why children reach their milestones at different stages. For each individual sign of the zodiac I have discussed the three main elements that determine your child's personality. These are the Sun, Moon and ascendant. 'Your child's will' refers to the Sun in your child's horoscope, 'Your child's emotions' to the Moon sign and 'First impressions' to your child's ascendant sign. It is best to read all three for a better overall picture of your individual child's makeup.

Additional factors to take into consideration are how the planets affect our children and how, when any two planets make a connection, they affect and influence each other. This is especially of interest when looking at the primary components of the horoscope, the Sun, Moon and the point directly overhead (midheaven, or MC) and rising (ascendant) at the time of birth.

The MC and ascendant, also known as the angles, are of particular importance. It has been shown that planets rising (on the ascendant) or culminating (on the MC) at the time of birth have the greatest impact on career choice and success in our chosen fields.

We are all unique individuals and as such follow our own drumbeat. Many factors help to shape us: heredity, socio-economic status, culture, religion and nature each play their part. The natural side of life follows the rhythm of the seasons as we travel around the Sun, along with the other planets. Our combined journey impacts on everything taking part and we are influenced by all of the planets. When we understand and follow these natural rhythms ourselves, life becomes clearer and simpler and we find we are better able to reach our goals.

Note: if you wish to see your child's full horoscope, you can do so without charge on my website, *www.heavenschild.com.au*. To help you understand your child's chart, I have listed at the end of this book all the symbols used.

your child's potential

Your child's horoscope can reveal many things that will give you a head start from the moment of your child's birth. Why do some babies need lots of physical contact, while others don't enjoy being held tightly? Why do some children go to bed and straight to sleep every night, while others are still wide awake long after you are ready for bed? Why are some kids easygoing and have no problem making friends, while others prefer their own company? Your child's horoscope answers these questions and more. As well as showing possible areas of conflict or difficulty for your child, their horoscope also provides solutions, so you can put in place strategies to help overcome problems before or as they arise.

It's much easier to be a better and more informed parent and to know how to protect and nurture your child when you understand what's best for them. Through your child's horoscope a trained astrologer can see at a glance if your child is more likely to have allergies or susceptibility to other health issues. They can also see if your child is likely to have fears or phobias, and how and when these are likely to manifest. Just as your child's genes will determine the colour of their eyes, skin or hair, so their birth chart shows personality characteristics, what type of activities they prefer, even their food preferences.

As you will see, astrology gives us wonderful insights into the various stages of childhood development and why these stages occur when they do. Most people have heard of the 'terrible twos', for example, but *Star Parenting* explains why this occurs at the age of two and not three or four. Why do babies become 'clingy' at around six months and why do some children find socialising so easy while others have so much difficulty in this area? These quesions are all answered in commonsense and easy-to-understand language that puts you in the position of knowing rather than wondering.

You will also gain insights about yourself as a parent. Why does one child always seem to know which buttons to push? Why does it seem easier or harder to relate to particular children? With *Star Parenting* you will understand more about psychological motivators and how to work with them. These insights will help you improve your parenting skills, create a better relationship with your child and put your son or daughter on the path that will unlock their hidden potential. Wouldn't it be great to know from the time your child was very young the career path they will be most suited to, and to be able to put the right tools at their fingertips from a young age? With *Star Parenting* you will be in a much more informed position to do just that. Whether your child is a potential artist, scientist, teacher, lawyer, musician or plumber, you will be able to provide them with activities that will suit their needs.

I have been at the births of all of my grandchildren. As I was aware of where the planets were during each labour, I was able to predict the major characteristics of my grandchildren even before they were born. I was able to tell my daughter, Caitlin, that her baby girl would be a fussy feeder, so she didn't feel a failure when breastfeeding proved difficult. As a result, Caitlin was able to utilise feeding practices that suited her daughter's individual needs. Olivia is now a happy four-year-old with a healthy appetite. Too often, parents experience feelings of guilt and failure when there is a problem. But rather than failing to be a 'good' parent, it is usually simply a case of not understanding their child's needs.

Astrology is brilliant at helping parents fill in the gaps. It's not surprising that astrology is so helpful; it is the oldest science known to man. Most of our 'modern' sciences developed from the study of the heavens. The ancients living in Mesopotamia created the longest continuous record of scientific observation in human history, spanning several thousand years. Their observations not only plotted the movement of heavenly bodies but also recorded daily the events that coincided with these movements: as above, so below. The modern astrologer draws on over four thousand years of accumulated learning when interpreting the position of the Earth and other planets at any given moment in time, for example, in the birth horoscope.

Coming from a large family and myself the mother of seven children, I have had plenty of experience with family dynamics and how different individual children can be. But it wasn't until I began a study of astrology that I gained the insights I had been missing. Knowing the nuances of your child's personality traits, their individual potential, and the timing of their stages of development is something all parents struggle with, and astrology provides the key to understanding.

For example, you probably wouldn't be aware that your child's ability to communicate—when they will utter their first word, and so on—is connected with the movement of the planet Mercury in their chart. The development of motor skills—when your child takes their first steps—is related to the planet Mars, while specific likes and dislikes can be traced to the placement of Venus and the Moon at the time of their birth.

Star Parenting goes into much greater depth than the popular Sun sign—more commonly called star sign—astrology. In fact, it will plainly show you why your child may not be, say, a typical Aries or Taurus. It will instead show you who they really are.

One of the criticisms levelled at astrology is that it only uses one of twelve Sun signs to describe an individual's personality. In fact, each person's horoscope is a unique combination of Sun, Moon and the other eight planets in our solar system. Simply by adding the Moon sign to the Sun sign we go from twelve to 144 possible 'personality types'. When we add the other planets, such complex combinations are created that it makes each moment in time unique; the horoscope for a birth can never be repeated.

The advantage of astrology over any of the 'personality' tests is that it offers a clear map for our life course, from the moment we draw our first breath. You, the parent, will have this advantage: knowing and understanding your child's predisposition, you can create a world that will nurture and encourage them in safety and comfort.

You will be able to clearly discern their different developmental stages and why these occur at different times, understanding that each child operates on their own schedule. In a fast-moving, constantly changing world, *Star Parenting* offers you the tools to work with your child in a relaxed and easy manner, helping them achieve their full potential in life.

What kind of parent are you?

Before we get to know your child's horoscope, it's useful to know where your own strengths and weaknesses lie in the area of parenting. So take a look at the following section to see where you are at. How you react as a parent will also depend on what sign your child is. Knowing the possibilities and potential flashpoints will help you be the best mum or dad possible.

The Aries parent

Being under the rulership of the planet Mars, Aries embodies the fiery characteristics of the red planet. It is also a fire sign and of the *cardinal* or initiating quality. Arians are active by nature, and this includes their parenting style. As initiators, this is what they do best, leaving the finishing to someone else. The Aries parent takes to parenting in the same way as they approach anything in life: head-on. As Aries can themselves be very childlike, they generally relate quite well to children. As parents, they actively encourage their children to be involved in physical pastimes. Like the Aries child, they can be quick to flare up, but just as quickly let anger go.

The Aries father can be a little overbearing, leading by example rather than words. More sensitive children can feel intimidated and this dad needs to learn to read the signals coming from his children. However, he will be warm and affectionate to his children, and enjoy being an active participant in their lives. He can be a little like a supplanted older sibling when a new baby first arrives, and still needs to feel he is important to his partner. There can be a tendency with the Aries father to not know when too much of a good thing is harmful, such as a tickle match just before bedtime. Try to keep the more exuberant play for before bath- or dinnertime and try more gentle play or a bedtime story just before bed.

The Aries mother doesn't mollycoddle her children. Taking care of the practicalities, she expects a certain level of independence and self-sufficiency in her children and is not overly fussy. She will be a firm disciplinarian, expecting obedience. She will teach her children to believe in magic and fairytales, and she will enjoy walking in her child's fantasy. Like the Aries father, this mother needs to be aware that her sometimes brash manner can be upsetting to her more sensitive children, in particular those born under the water signs.

The challenge for Aries parents is to remember that they are the parent, as sometimes they can behave more like the child. Aries parents should endeavour to curb some of the Aries impulsiveness, which can be unnerving to the more sensitive child or the child who likes predictability and routine. Join your children in their fantasy and creative play but remember to set the boundaries and keep them. Your children will look to you for guidance and reassurance as they grow. Encourage their independence but don't push them too soon. Try to have some sort of routine, even if it is only a loose one.

The Taurus parent

Taurus is under the rulership of Venus, the planet associated with love and sensuality. It is also of the element earth and a fixed sign. This gives Taurus a reputation for stability, or, in the eyes of some, stubbornness. Calm and solid: this is the Taurean, until something or someone gets them riled. Taurus enjoys the simple comforts of life, good food, the peace of the countryside, a warm bed and lots of hugs. Generally a homebody, they fall into the role of parenthood without too much fuss, as long as they are able to preserve a semblance of their normal routine.

The Taurus father will be openly loving and patient and willing to spend time teaching their child anything he feels is important, and a lot of these lessons will revolve around the need for security. He administers discipline firmly but fairly. It takes a lot to rile this parent and others may be amazed at the restraint he shows when trying to instil respect and tolerance into his offspring. There can be a tendency to rule with an iron fist and be inflexible. He will be warm and sympathetic when needed but also able to give sound practical advice.

The Taurus mother is in her element with the baby and toddler in her life but may have difficulty when that cute cuddly little being turns into the hormone-fuelled teenager. Partly due to her love of beauty and peace, the Taurus mother can be too strict and demanding. She expects her children to be obedient, and can become the angry bull if she feels her discipline is being thwarted. She will not tolerate laziness in her children and gives them a strong sense of responsibility.

The challenge for the Taurean parent is to rise above the natural inclination to be overcautious and overprotective of their children. It is also important to learn flexibility and that there can be other perspectives outside yours. Allow your children some freedom; otherwise they can feel they are being suffocated.

The Gemini parent

Being a mutable air sign, under the governorship of Mercury, Gemini is a social and an intellectual sign. This creates a tendency to spend a lot of time 'in the head'. Gemini parents are great at coming up with answers but the tendency to avoid emotional situations can leave their children feeling emotionally abandoned. Geminis tend to express their ever-present 'inner child' when interacting with children, and the Gemini parent ensures their child has access to any number of extracurricular activities but can feel totally at a loss when faced with their child's emotional demands. Socially conscious, they will entertain the neighbourhood, but may fall down in providing one-on-one time with their own child.

The Gemini father does not generally make a good disciplinarian and although he is unlikely to lose his temper physically, his natural cutting wit can do serious damage to the developing young ego of his child. Consistency is something Geminis can have a problem with, yet children need consistency in order to feel secure. Dad will be in his element being a big kid with his children and will be quite happy to get on the floor and play and help his children to be relaxed with themselves. At the same time, though, he needs to be able to provide them with stability and security.

The Gemini mother also relishes the fun side of parenthood. She will instil a sense of independence into her brood but they may feel a lack of stability. This mother will be concerned with her child's academic achievements but needs to guard against this being the only way her child can gain her approval. She can spend hours lost in imagination and play with her children, encouraging their minds to expand, which can also be helpful for bonding. But it is equally important to give them a routine and security.

The challenge for the Gemini parent is to be consistent with discipline and responsibility. The natural tendency is to be fluid and changeable, but children need firm boundaries and security. Consistency offers children security.

The cancer parent

Cancer is a cardinal water sign and under the rulership of the Moon. The Cancerian is the natural sign of mother and home and, as such, generally makes a caring, if somewhat unpredictable, parent. Good humour and a wonderful ability to mimic make them fun parents. Sensitive both to their own and others' needs, Cancerians are generally concerned for the wellbeing of those they care about. As a parent they can be controlling, born from their own fears. 'Don't climb that tree; you might fall', is a likely response to the sight of their child attempting independence and expanding their horizons.

The Cancer father is caring, gentle and sympathetic, has a great sense of humour and enjoys the opportunity to play. Even the local kids will beat a path to his door. He is proud and fiercely protective of his children, ultimately patient and is genuinely concerned for their wellbeing. The problems manifest with this father when the children get older and begin to show their independence. Cancer needs to be needed. His love and concern, while admirable, can be seen as controlling by his children. The art is to find that fine line and not step over it too often.

The Cancer mother creates a warm and comfortable environment for her children. She may not be the neatest housekeeper, but the home will always be welcoming, with wonderful aromas emanating from the kitchen as she tempts her brood with her latest culinary efforts. The Cancer mother tends to resort to comfort-feeding to solve all ills and this can result in an overfed child physically and a mother who is overly manipulative or clingy when it comes to her children. Emotional manipulation can be the price for comfort.

The challenge for Cancer parents is to move beyond their own fear base and allow their child some freedom. It is important to allow the child to develop into his or her own person and eventually to leave the safety and comfort of the nest.

The Leo parent

Leo is a fixed fire sign, ruled by the Sun. As the Sun is the centre of the solar system, many Leos also consider themselves to be the centre, around which everything else revolves. Like their animal namesake, the Leo parent will defend his or her young to the death. Leos take great pride in their children and woe betide any outsider who dares attack them. When they become parents they are warm and loving without smothering their children, generally encouraging them to be independent.

The Leo father demands respect from his children but does not make a very good disciplinarian. Again, look to the animal namesake; it is the lioness who is responsible for the raising of the offspring, while the male lies around demanding the adoration of his pride. He can be a fun dad, affectionate and adoring, but is too easily manipulated—especially by his daughters, who will have his measure early on, knowing that the right flattery will almost guarantee them what they want.

The Leo mother will be the disciplinarian and can often quieten her rowdy brood with just a look. She will frolic with her children and give love generously. She is not always able to clearly see the faults in her children, but when she does she is very strict and expects obedience. She will also demand certain standards to be kept, especially in public. Even though she is firm, she is also generous and can go overboard with little luxuries. This mother would protect her children with her life but does not smother them, keeping an eye on them from a safe distance, ready to pounce if the need arises.

The challenge for Leo parents is to move outside their own
ego and see their children realistically; to satisfy the child's
needs rather than the parent's desire for approval.

The Virgo parent

Virgo is an earth sign and like its airy counterpart Gemini, is
of the mutable quality and under the rulership of Mercury. Even
though of the earth element, it is also a mental or intellectual
sign. Where Gemini resides in the realm of ideas and possibilities,
the earth influence makes Virgo more practical with a desire to
make ideas realities. Virgos are also known for their concerns
with health matters; as parents, this preoccupation and their
attention to the finer details turn parenthood into a chore
rather than a pleasure, if taken too far.

The Virgo father is a conscientious parent who enjoys
teaching his children new skills. He will sit with his children,
assisting them with their homework and he will encourage
them to develop hobbies. There will be an emphasis on
intellectual pursuits and this father will also instil a firm base
for ethics and moral behaviour. Not a father to spoil his
children, he will provide a secure and loving environment
with firm discipline and respect for the rules. His downfall is
in physically expressing his love, which does not come naturally
to him.

The Virgo mother is a firm but fair disciplinarian, taking
good care of her child's physical, moral and educational needs.
Like the Virgo father, she may find it more difficult to take
care of the emotional needs of her child but will provide
warm and gentle affection when comfortable and relaxed

within herself. Able to show the softer side to her children, she can be quite funny and entertaining. The child of the Virgo mother may visit the doctor more than the average child but will develop healthy habits and an understanding of their own body.

> *The challenge* for a Virgo parent is to relax and enjoy the experience, and not to dwell on health issues that may give rise to children being overly concerned with their own wellbeing. Teach your child healthy habits but don't become obsessive.

The Libra parent

Libra is a cardinal air sign under the rulership of Venus. This sign has a sense of aesthetics, enjoying good music, food and the arts. It is also the sign that most signifies relationships. Librans generally prefer company to solitude. As parents, they educate their children in the social graces: being polite and when to say and do the 'right thing'. As the diplomat of the zodiac they will mediate on behalf of their child and try to instil a sense of justice and fair play. Their tendency to keep the peace at all costs can create a lack of true discipline.

The Libra father is generally a calm character who rarely shows his ruffled feathers. He will administer discipline fairly and with logic. He can bore the pants off the youngsters with his lectures but will enjoy taking them on trips to the local museum or art gallery and honing their social skills in group situations. He will entertain their friends with grace and style and be willing to pull his weight in school and community organisations.

The Libra mother will make sure that her children have a neat and tidy living environment. She sees her primary role as preparing her children to take their place in society. Good manners, correct speech and diplomacy are high on her list, along with a good education. 'Make sure you have clean underwear on in case you get hit by a bus' is the cry the child may hear on leaving the house. Keeping up appearances is important to the Libra mother.

> *The challenge* for the Libra parent is to accept that sometimes tough decisions need to be made. You may even need to take sides, and sometimes your child may not like you. This is part of the parenting territory, but your child will still love you, and, more importantly, develop respect for you.

The Scorpio parent

Scorpio is a fixed water sign ruled by Mars. It is a sign that does nothing by halves and takes life fairly seriously. This sign is recognised for its passion, courage under fire and willingness to go where angels fear to tread. As parents, Scorpios are fearless when it comes to protecting their children: heaven help anyone who threatens their wellbeing. Scorpio parents are generally firm with discipline but can have a blind spot to their children's faults.

The Scorpio father can be overbearing and wield his authority in a high-handed manner. His children will have no doubt as to who is in charge. They will feel secure with his strength and conviction but may rail against the tight yoke they feel he places on them. He can be light-hearted and enjoy playing with his children but with this father there are very firm boundaries that must not be crossed. He gives his children a sense of purpose and encourages them to be independent and stand up for themselves, knowing that he is standing right behind.

The Scorpio mother, although not the most tender caregiver, gives her children the feeling of security. She will encourage her children in their endeavours, especially if they show a talent in a particular area. This is the mum who willingly takes her child to the local pool every morning at 5 am for training, or to ballet or music classes five days a week. She makes a good confidante and her children will recognise this quality, along with her willingness to hear them out without judgment. There are usually good lines of communication in this mother–child relationship. Her children will also recognise her strength and wisdom, which she has usually gained from experience.

The challenge for Scorpio is to be realistic regarding their children and not allow jealousy and competitiveness to build enmity within their social circle. Life is not a competition.

The Sagittarius parent

Sagittarius is a mutable fire sign ruled by the planet Jupiter. This is the sign of the wanderer and the eternally curious.

Sagittarians love to experience life and learn as much as they can about their world and about others. As parents they encourage their children to follow their lead, discovering and investigating their environment. Not a cloying parent, they are quite the opposite. Their children may complain of a lack of closeness and security but they will also learn independence, curiosity about the world and to aim high and wide.

The Sagittarius father may not be the doting daddy to the baby or toddler; in fact, he can find this stage quite a puzzle. However, once his children are old enough to join him on his escapades, it becomes a different story. This dad generally becomes closer to his children the older they get, and, unlike some of the other signs, is unfazed by teenage tantrums. His brutal frankness can be unnerving for the more sensitive child but his sense of humour will usually get him out of trouble.

The Sagittarius mother would rather be a friend than parent to her children. She can be so busy with her own pursuits that she is unaware of her children's needs, and her own need for freedom and independence does not make for a security-rich environment for her child. If she is aware of her own needs and is able to balance these with her child's needs, a great relationship can result as she teaches her children to be independent, free-thinking souls, with a wide range of interests and experiences.

The challenge for Sagittarius is to remember to be a parent first. Discipline is not a strong point and this parent finds it difficult to be consistent. Decide on the most important issues and be firm in those areas.

The capricorn parent

Capricorn is a cardinal earth sign ruled by Saturn. The business sign of the zodiac, Capricorn tends to take a businesslike approach to most things in life, including parenting. They are generally efficient and well-organised individuals until life impinges and throws them into chaos. Generally a resilient sign, they bounce back quite well, once everything is under their control again. There will be lists stuck to the fridge door with all of the chores, homework schedules, sports training, and so on. Capricorn parents are the rock upon which the child can depend for all practicalities, but when it comes to handing out parental affection, they may be cool.

The Capricorn father is a strong disciplinarian and likes to be the boss. He will not tolerate backchat and may seem overly strict or even old-fashioned to his children. He will provide them with stability and everything they need, although not always what they want. This dad expects obedience and respect and instils these qualities in his children. Not prone to frivolity, the Capricorn dad tends to take life too seriously. Children can be the perfect lightener, bringing him out of his shell and teaching him that life is not all responsibility but can be fun as well.

The Capricorn mother has a connection to tradition and is also a mother who likes to be involved in the community. She will tend to have a busy schedule and will incorporate her children's requirements into this. She will teach her children respect for their elders and tradition and expect them to behave appropriately. She will also instil a sense of economy that may border on miserliness, insisting that full value be obtained from everything, including wearing clothing until it is absolutely worn out.

> *The challenge* for the Capricorn parent is to provide their child with nurturance. If necessary, block out a few hours each week in your diary that is just for your child; not for a scheduled activity but for spontaneous fun.

The Aquarius parent

Aquarius is a fixed air sign also under the domain of Saturn. This is the sign of universal brotherhood: the Aquarian can often be seen at the forefront of a cause fighting for the underdog. Such endeavours appeal to their sense of fairness, though at the same time they maintain their distance. They are great at loving the world, but not so good in one-on-one relationships. As parents they will teach their children to respect others and to be community-minded. The Aquarian would like to be a 'friend' to their children but needs first to provide security; friendship comes later.

The Aquarius father will have a fairly relaxed attitude to parenting and seems to handle most situations with ease. Part of the reason he appears to do so well is that he is often detached from the reality around him. He will encourage his children in their endeavours, try to make it to all the soccer games, swimming carnivals, and so on, yet is likely to be late for his daughter's wedding. His children may see him as an enigma and may never really get to know him intimately, unless they can somehow join him in his own world.

The Aquarius mother is not physically demonstrative, and is flustered by the demands of a baby or small child. She will become involved in education and extracurricular activities, but will expect independence from her children. She may find the more emotional side of parenting a conundrum. She will gladly give time to help with school projects and will never speak down to children. Where discipline is concerned, the Aquarius mother will be quite tolerant of her children's behaviour as long as they are honest. This household may seem very chaotic to the outside world but, while not the tightest ship in the fleet, it will be fun, with a sympathetic and non-judgmental outlook.

The challenge for the Aquarius parent is to overcome their fear of intimacy and teach their child the joy of a close relationship with another individual.

The Pisces parent

The last of the twelve zodiac signs is Pisces, a mutable water sign ruled by Jupiter. Pisces is the empathetic sign of the zodiac and recognised for its sensitivity. However, the symbol of Pisces is two fish swimming in opposite directions: while one may be the gentle guppy, the other can be a barracuda. There is a tough side to this gentle sign. It may not show often, but threaten Pisces' loved ones and you will see it. Pisceans tend to be sensitive to the needs and emotions of others and can be overwhelmed when there are no barriers.

The Pisces father will always have an open mind, and a shoulder for his children to lean on. This is not a judgmental sign and as such can lack discrimination, especially with their own children. This is the dad who will tell wonderful bedtime stories of princes and frogs and good overcoming evil; who will teach them to paint using their feet on a canvas spread on the floor and allow them to express their inner selves. This household will revolve more on communal principles, where everything belongs to everyone. Discipline can also be lacking and boring things like homework may not be a high priority.

The Pisces mother has an in-built radar for detecting the wounded soul. Where other mothers may be good at putting Band-Aids on the scraped knee, this one knows how to put them on the heart. She can sprinkle fairy dust to ward off bad dreams and fill her child's world with fantasy and magic. She will bolster their self-confidence and convince them they can be whoever they want to be. She may have difficulty, however, in setting boundaries and teaching self-discipline.

The challenge for the Pisces parent is to create suitable boundaries and love their children without becoming dependent on them to fill any void in their own lives.

HOW you relate to your child

'While we try to teach our children all about life,
our children teach us what life is all about.'

Angela Schwindt

Being a parent is one of the most rewarding, and stressful,
of all occupations. When you hold that tiny bundle in your
arms for the first time, you are filled with such deep emotions:
overwhelming feelings of love and protection, as well as the
fear of making a mistake that may mark your child for life.

Your child's early years will influence their health and
happiness as an adult. Studies show that the first two years
of life lay the foundations for how we behave, think and even
love as adults. This happens when your child is too young to
talk or tell you their needs, so it helps to know as much as
you can, as early as possible, about your child.

> The good news is that there is no such thing as a
> 'perfect parent' or the 'perfect child'.

To thrive, our children need love and acceptance of who
they are. They also need our time, and to feel special. When

you know what your child is likely to enjoy, it is easier for you to encourage them in their choices. You know how to make the most of your time with them, not by scheduling their every waking moment but by offering meaningful activities balanced with free time to be 'kids'.

Most of us will experience feeling like a square peg in a round hole at some stage in our lives. We each have natural abilities and talents and the more we are able to express our own unique personality, the less square we become and the closer we get to being a well-rounded human being.

All parents want the best for their child, which goes without saying. Often what parents want most for their child is something lacking in their own childhood.

The parent who lacked material possessions will shower their child with gifts. However, while this makes the parent feel good, it may not be what the child needs or wants.

A child's needs are fairly simple. Love and acceptance are at the top of the list. It is important that you love, nurture and honour your child for who they are, not what you want them to be. A child will do anything to receive your approval, but this may not be the best way for them to develop into who they are meant to be. The boy who loves music, but knows his father wants him to be a star on the football field, will punish himself week after week to gain approval by playing a sport he hates. Rather than setting yourself up for the inevitable rebellion, accept and love your child for who they are, and everyone wins.

Your child needs you for guidance. They will have their peers as friends but look to you for the boundaries and encouragement they need to learn to become a part of society. Your responsibility is not to be your child's best friend but to be your child's parent.

Parent-child combinations

Fire parent

Aries, Leo and Sagittarius make up the fire trinity; these parents are dynamic, playful and imaginative. They will be openly affectionate and demonstrative, genuinely enjoying the company of children. They can lack a sense of practicality and generally are not good with routine or time management. They believe in magic and will endeavour to pass this on to their children.

- **Fire parent with a fire child:** This dynamic, if somewhat fiery and tempestuous, relationship can be enjoyed by both parties. A shared enjoyment of physical activities can be a bonding point, as will their optimism and belief in the magic of the world. Problems can arise when the parent identifies too much with the child, denying the child space to be their own person. Idealising (or idolising) each other is wonderful until the statue falls off the pedestal.
- **Fire parent with an earth child:** This can be mutually beneficial with the fire parent bringing spontaneity and magic to the earth child, who in turn can teach the parent stability and patience. It is important for the fire parent

to respect their earth child's need for security and routine. The fire parent may find it hard to understand their child's need for sameness and their difficulty in believing in things that are not tangible. The earth child needs to physically experience something for it to be real but the fire parent can help teach them about the intangible and imagination.

- **Fire parent with an air child:** This relationship embodies the melding of ideas and imagination. Many a long discussion over the dinner table on just about any subject imaginable can be one scenario. This relationship can run into difficulty when both parent and child are living in the realm of possibility rather than reality. The fire parent will encourage the dreams of the air child, as well as their freedom and independence.

- **Fire parent with a water child:** This is probably the most difficult child for the fire parent to understand, as where fire is passionate, this child is emotional. The fire parent may not understand the sensitivity of their little water baby. Fire and water combined create steam and this can well describe what happens when these two find themselves together. The fire parent should try to be objective and accept that we are all different.

Earth parent

Capricorn, Taurus and Virgo are the earth trinity and these parents are practical, security-conscious and organised. They take care of the essentials in life, will be physically aware and give their children a firm foundation and material grounding.

They may lack imagination and spontaneity and be too rigid in their parenting for some children.

- **Earth parent with an earth child:** This combination provides both parties with security and stability. The child depends on the parent for their protection and wellbeing and will usually be a relatively easy child for the earth parent to understand. The combination can lack creativity and imagination.
- **Earth parent with a fire child:** The fire child can be a handful for the earth parent but perseverance will pay off in the long run. The earth parent will tear their hair out at the fire child's lack of discipline and inability to focus on the material world. The child, on the other hand, can feel the parent is stifling their creativity and imagination. Earth puts out fire and the risk in this relationship is the parent stifling an essential part of their child's nature. The plus is that this combination mixes the realm of possibilities and dreams with the ability to create reality.
- **Earth parent with an air child:** This is another relationship where the child can feel stifled and misunderstood. It can be a clash of matter and thought where the child deals in reality and the parent in ideas. In this case the parent needs to show patience and explain everything, as reason will win out over force.
- **Earth parent with a water child:** This can be a comfortable relationship with one needing security and the other wanting to give the same. The earth parent may find the water child's emotions overwhelming at times but if you

can remember to give comfort in times of need, you will find things settle quickly.

Air parent

The air trinity consists of Aquarius, Gemini and Libra. These parents can spend hours talking to their children and trying to take a logical approach. This is often lost on the children, who can be anything but logical. Advice to the air parent, if you wish to follow the book, make sure your child has read the same edition.

- **Air parent with an air child:** This household has a lot of noise. There will be constant chatter and exchange of ideas and experiences; a television in one room, stereo in the next and the radio blaring in another, all eliciting comments and discussion. What can be lacking are grounding and a sense of practicality.
- **Air parent with an earth child:** The air parent may find the earth child's need for physical connection puzzling. Words are not enough, this child learns through experience and much of that is through the senses: taste, touch, sight, sound and smell. In this household there can be an auditory blowout with not enough attention given to the other senses. The air parent needs to ensure that all of the senses receive equal attention.
- **Air parent with a fire child:** This can be an interesting mix and is usually compatible, although a little crazy. Again, neither has practicality as their forte, and while

they can have fun and come up with fantastic ideas, they may not achieve a great deal unless there is some earth in the charts. This can be an inspirational mix and extremely creative.

- **Air parent with a water child:** The overriding logic of the air parent can be lost on the sensitive, emotional water child. This parent should set aside the need for everything to make sense when dealing with this child and acknowledge that sometimes there is no explanation. Give the hugs and reassurance that your child is seeking and all will be well.

water parent

The water trinity encompasses Pisces, Cancer and Scorpio. This group parents by feeling. They can make empathetic and understanding parents who are always willing to provide a shoulder to lean on when needed. These parents have a highly developed sixth sense—which they should trust—when it comes to their children.

- **Water parent with a water child:** Creative, intuitive and spiritually inclined, this combination can create the genius or the martyr, depending on other planetary factors. Tea and sympathy can be good initially but too much can lead to wallowing in past hurts instead of moving forward and getting on with life.
- **Water parent with an air child:** The freedom-seeking air child can be overwhelmed and closed in by the emotional water parent. They can also learn that emotions are not

something to be afraid of. The need for logical explanations can have the water parent in a quandary; they know that not all things can be explained but try telling that to an air child.

- **Water parent with an earth child:** Water and earth are a fertile combination as each provides what the other needs for growth. This parent can give inspiration that the child can turn into reality with the right support. The child may at times despair of the parent's lack of practicality, but generally this is an easy combination.

- **Water parent with a fire child:** This can be a testing relationship for both parties, but it also has benefits. The fire child's willingness to take risks and step into unknown territory can help the parent to overcome some of their own fears, if they are willing to follow. The fire child learns from this parent to be more aware of others' feelings and that there are other perspectives on life.

your child

A child's horoscope is their individual life map, as complex and individual as they are. It reveals, from the moment of birth, what your child requires from life and what he or she has to offer.

Most people are familiar with their Sun sign which describes overall characteristics, but horoscopes are about a whole lot more. They give us clues to the smallest details, from food preferences to sleeping habits and even musical taste. Once you're aware of these details, you know your child's challenges and potentials, where their comfort zone begins and ends and where they might need a little more support and encouragement.

Where the planets are placed in your child's chart at the moment of their birth will influence not only their personality but also their direction in life, their passions, their comfort zones and their challenges. Here is some information to help you understand these possibilities.

your child's life purpose

The Sun, Moon, Mercury, Venus and Mars, ascendant and midheaven (also known as MC, or *medium caeli*, which is

Latin for 'middle of the sky') are known as the personal points. These parts of the horoscope are the fastest moving and are 'personal' to the individual. In order to share an ascendant degree, two babies would need to be born within four minutes of each other, in the exact same location. These personal planets will be the main developmental factors in your child's early years, with their cycles marking the development of language, motor and social skills. The personal planets also play a major role in what is known as individuation—or awareness of the self as a separate individual—mobility and self-assertion.

Meeting the world

Your child's ascendant, also known as their rising sign, is the section of the heavens that is rising over the eastern horizon at the exact moment of their birth. Some say this represents the soul's arrival on earth and connects us to our world. In your child's horoscope it also represents their physical body and shows how they meet the world head-on. It is the mask we wear when we first meet people and is the filter through which all the planetary influences are expressed. It acts as a modifier for all other planets and points within the chart. The ascendant will be modified by any planet making contact, particularly by a planet that is rising at the time of birth.

The opposite point is the descendant, or setting point. This is the relating axis and tells much about the types of people your child will attract into their life and are attracted to.

Career choices

Your child's midheaven, or MC, is the point that is directly overhead at the time of your child's birth. The midheaven represents your child's aspirations and public persona, and will show their likely career choices. Directly opposite this point is the *Imum coeli*, or IC, which represents their family, where they come from, their roots, the type of home they prefer and what comforts them.

Aims and ambitions

In your child's horoscope, the Sun represents their ego, where and how they would like to shine. It's that individual identity that looks for the light and to be recognised. The Sun represents your child's aims and ambitions. It shows where and how they will grow as an individual. When your child is very young their Sun is only glimpsed occasionally. The more secure and confident your child becomes, the more their Sun will shine. Their self-expression will be modified by any of the following planets in close contact in their chart.

Emotions and habits

The Moon represents your child's emotions and instinctual responses, how they respond in emotional situations. As the Moon rules infancy and early childhood, your child's instincts and emotions will be most apparent during their early years. The Moon is aware of different emotional environments and needs. It adapts and adjusts its behaviour until everything feels comfortable and secure. It shows what your child needs for emotional security and how to obtain it. The expression of a child's emotion depends on which other planets are in close contact to their Moon.

communication

Mercury, the messenger of the gods, represents your child's thought, logic and speech. It shows how we process information and communicate with others.

Mercury lightens and brightens whatever it contacts. It makes children inquisitive; that's why Mercurial children (and adults) enjoy learning and gathering information. If this is your child, they usually enjoy reading, working on puzzles and games, including computer games, that stretch their mental boundaries. Your child will also appreciate good conversation, and can be a real little chatterbox. Mercury is most at home in the air signs: Aquarius, Gemini and Libra. Fairytale writer Hans Christian Andersen and poet T.S. Eliot are well-known examples of the mercurial personality. Storytelling is a very mercurial art, especially for those with a well-placed Mercury.

Friendship

Venus, the goddess of love and the most beautiful of the visible planets, is associated with love, friendship and the arts in the birth horoscope. The position of this planet shows how your child relates to others, the type of friends they will attract, their tastes in art and music and how important these things will be to your child.

When in close proximity to the Sun, Moon or angles (midheaven or ascendant), Venus gives a gentleness, a love of beauty and connection to the material. These are the children who enjoy art and music from an early age. The great painter Vincent Van Gogh had a prominent Venus.

If Venus is in an earth sign in your child's chart, they will love sensuous things and these boys and girls are very tactile and need to touch, smell and taste everything. Venus also brings beauty. Babies with a prominent Venus quite often have a dimple or two. If this is your child, they will have a very disarming smile and be a little charmer. A strong Venus gives charisma, so people are drawn to them as they were to former US president John F. Kennedy, and Hollywood's 'fairytale princess' Grace Kelly.

A strong Venus will make your child very sociable. They will enjoy sharing time with friends and family, and tend to take on the role of peacemaker. These little politicians and lawyers in training can also begin disputes in order to have an opportunity to practise their diplomacy.

Assertiveness

This planet, associated with the ancient god of war, represents our ability to assert ourselves. Along with the Sun, it focuses us on our physical wellbeing and stamina.

Mars in your child's chart adds energy, forcefulness, assertiveness and sporting prowess. Children with a strong

Mars are full of life and can wear out even the fittest of parents. They can be perpetually on the move and need plenty of physical activity to burn off all their energy. If they don't they can become angry and aggressive. Quick to anger, they are just as quick to forgive and forget.

It is no surprise that champion golfer Tiger Woods has Mars in a prominent position at the top of his horoscope. Francis Ford Coppola, the film director of *The Godfather* and *Apocalypse Now*, two movies with strong Martian themes, had Mars rising at the time of his birth.

Your Mars child can be accident-prone, as these boys and girls take on life full tilt. They may have trouble concentrating on tasks for any length of time. Direction of energy is the key for a happy little Martian.

peer group

The social planets, Jupiter and Saturn, help connect boys and girls to their peer group. Jupiter remains in a sign for approximately one year, while Saturn has an average stay of two and a half years. This means everyone in your child's immediate peer group, of the same age, will be influenced by these planets in the same way. On a larger scale it influences our social conscience, law-making and economic cycles, as well as our fashions, movies and television shows. Teachers in particular will be aware of this: my late husband, who was a high school teacher, quite often commented on certain years of students who were noted for particular behaviour patterns that persisted from kindergarten through to graduation. Many of my friends and family are teachers and they all see the connection, especially when I explain what the attitudes towards school and learning will be for any of these different groups.

Expanding horizons

Jupiter (Zeus) is the father of the gods and laws and social order. As the first of the 'social' planets, it influences how your child and their peers will relate to the world, education and their level of optimism. If they don't get enough of what they need, it can be difficult to find pleasure in life. Too much of a good thing can make them a manic personality. Jupiter represents a child's ability to take in new concepts. When well placed in a horoscope, it is the planet of the 'visionary'.

If your child has a strong Jupiter, they will be adventurous and outgoing and have a strong desire to learn and explore. These boys and girls are interested in the spiritual side of life, and will tend to ask questions such as, 'What is God?', 'What happens when we die?' and 'Why do people have different coloured skin?'. Well before their third birthday they are curious about life and people, philosophy and religion. They will constantly be seeking knowledge, understanding and experience, hungry for the myriad of rich cultural and religious experiences that await them. Space pioneer John Glenn and movie hero Indiana Jones are great examples of Jupiter in action. The Jupiter child has an open, curious and broad mind, and a well-developed sense of humour. Bill Cosby used his Jupiterian humour to amuse millions.

Keep a wide range of books on hand for Jupiter boys and girls. Nature excursions or a trip to the local shops enable them to do what they love: meet new people and enjoy different experiences. Your Jupiter child may grow into another Jacques Cousteau, the world's greatest ocean explorer, who had Jupiter rising at birth. Whichever path they choose, life with a Jupiter-blessed child will never be dull.

Responsibility

Saturn, the second of the 'social' planets, is considered the boundary rider of the solar system and is therefore associated with limitation, boundaries, practicality and our sense of reality. It also helps us to make our dreams real. As the planet of structure, Saturn influences your child's skeletal system and skin according to the ancient traditions and therefore governs structure and boundaries. Where Saturn appears in the horoscope, it shows where your child will tend to strive the most and where they feel compelled to try even harder.

The Saturn child will tend to be more serious and grown-up than their years would indicate. These children tend to be referred to as 'old souls in young bodies'. Saturn allows boys and girls to focus, so they see clearly the path they wish to tread. It can lead to sullenness and depression if the child does not receive enough positive reinforcement. The child with a strong Saturn needs lots of reassurance and encouragement to counteract their belief they are not good enough. These children take on responsibility from a very young age, so parents need to watch they aren't burdening their child with too much responsibility. These children enjoy the company of adults and older children, and need to be encouraged to interact with their peer group. Saturn is also prominent in the charts of musicians and comedians and gives them a black or dry humour; Noel Coward, Charlie Chaplin, Bob Dylan, Woody Allen, Gene Wilder and John Belushi have all had a strong Saturn influence.

children of their generation

Uranus, Neptune and Pluto in a child's chart connect them to their generational group. Uranus is in the same sign for seven years, Neptune for fourteen years and Pluto can be in the same sign from ten to almost 30 years. These planets exert a much greater influence on the human race as a whole than on the individual. In the individual horoscope, their placement and closeness to your child's Sun or Moon shows how your child fits into their generation. Are they part of the collective, leaders of the pack, or do they prefer to buck the system?

Rebellion

The planet Uranus was discovered by telescope in 1781, during a century marked by the great change and upheaval of the industrial revolution and both the French and American revolutions. This planet shows us what separates one generation of children from their elders, how they express their individuality and their attitude to authority. This planet also represents progress and technology.

With Uranus we are moving into the 'outer limits' of our planetary system. Children with a personal connection to this planet tend to be more interested in the future than the here and now. These children are not lineal thinkers, their minds are zooming around any number of directions at any one time. As they grow, these girls and boys are in tune with the world around them and feel that nothing is impossible; they just haven't come across the right solution—yet. They can pull thoughts and solutions from the air. If your child has a personal planet close to this planet, they are likely to be leaders but will march to their own drumbeat, just like rock star Mick Jagger, revolutionary Karl Marx and comedian Spike Milligan. They may not sleep well as they have trouble shutting off their minds. A good, calm bedtime routine is a good habit to develop for these boys and girls.

creativity

Neptune, the water god, connects children to the subconscious or to the hidden aspects of life. Neptune is about feelings, intuition and creative impulses. It is the planet of spirit that ties us to the dreams we all have for the future. There is a very strong connection to psychic abilities and film, both of which flourished around the time of Neptune's discovery in 1846. Neptune features very prominently in the charts of many of Hollywood's most loved sons and daughters, as well as in those of musicians and artists, such as Michelangelo and Botticelli. It is connected to illusion—and delusion. This planet is also most associated with such screen and music legends as James Dean, Elvis Presley, Elizabeth Taylor and Marilyn Monroe. Neptune lends children the mystique needed to carry an image way beyond physical existence.

This is the planet of dreams and dreamers; that's why children with a strong Neptune can sometimes appear ethereal. They are very intuitive and live in a fantasy world. They tend to daydream a lot, and have 'imaginary friends': these children really do have the ability to tune into other realms. Very creative and artistic, these boys and girls enjoy music and art and need an outlet for their creativity and time alone. They pick up on the emotions of those around them. If you think you can fool these children, think again, for they intuitively know how you are feeling and thinking. Because of their sensitivity, the Neptune child needs to know how to build barriers around their emotions, as they are easily hurt. These children need to be eased gently into the realities of a sometimes harsh world. They are very empathetic and caring and need a spiritual element within their lives. There can also be confusion as to who they really are, so they may try out a number of different personalities on their journey to find their true self. There is also a connection to drugs and alcohol, which can explain why so many creative kids tend to lose themselves to substance abuse. It is wise to educate them early about the dangers of substance abuse.

Telling it like it is

Although now a 'dwarf planet', Pluto packs a power punch, as it is the planet of profound transformation. Pluto plumbs the depths of our subconscious. It creates the most change globally, and does so with remarkable predictability. Nations rise and fall in accordance with the cycles of this small but far from insignificant planet.

When connected to the Sun, Moon or ascendant in your child's horoscope, Pluto adds intensity to their personality. This is the child you find uncomfortable to lock gaze with, as you feel they are looking right into your soul, which in truth they are. There are no half-measures with the Pluto child: they are intense and full-on. Mary Shelley, writer and creator of the characters of Frankenstein and his monster, had a prominent Pluto, as did Picasso. There is no fooling this child, so don't even try: they need honesty above all else. Give your Plutonian child the cold hard facts of life and you will earn their respect, and enable them to experience life the way they were meant to.

Pluto children are not afraid to go where angels fear to tread. They will ask the questions everyone else is afraid to voice. This is the child who stops the conversation at Grandma's funeral by asking why the sole beneficiary, Aunty Joyce, looks so happy when everyone else is crying. Pop icon Madonna is an expression of Pluto. These children are very good at recognising the undercurrents of life, and the difference between spoken words and their underlying meaning. They also possess a magnetism that draws people of all descriptions to them, including those you would prefer they didn't attract. Their charter is to change the world through the explosive energy of a George W. Bush or to save the world like Superman Christopher Reeve, both born with Pluto rising.

your baby's first years

Developmental stages

How your child develops is influenced by the wider rhythm of the planets, and by their own birth map. That's why every girl and boy has their own rhythm. It is important to understand that an early walker doesn't make an Olympic athlete, or an early talker a Mensa candidate. The reverse is also true.

The order children come in the family also makes a difference. Firstborn children tend to reach milestones earlier than subsequent children. My second daughter was a very late walker, yet she became a very talented long-distance runner. Once she found her feet she was hard to stop. So it is important when learning about developmental milestones that you remember each child is unique.

Development of the individual

When a baby is born they have no awareness of being separate from the world around them, or being an individual. This awareness slowly develops during their first year of life and occurs in line with the Sun, which is about understanding our individual self or essence.

The first awareness of your baby's self usually occurs at around three months. This is when your baby becomes aware of their body, entranced by their own hands and fingers, feet and toes. From this awareness comes a curiosity about the things around them that are not a part of themself. At this stage your baby will begin reaching for toys, other people and their own reflection in the mirror. At this age, the Sun has moved one-quarter of the way around its first cycle reaching the first square, activating itself and the process of self-realisation.

At six months, the Sun has moved halfway in its first cycle and is now at the opposition point to its original position in your baby's chart. The opposition always brings in an awareness of 'others' as it is the furthest distance that can be achieved in the circle. This is when your baby can become very clingy, as they now realise they are a totally separate being and that those responsible for their care are not a part of them. This can be a major challenge in your baby's journey to becoming their own person.

How your child handles this time will depend on where the Sun is placed in their horoscope. The child with a strong Sun will find this process relatively easy. Babies with less favourable Sun placements in the chart may find this separation process more difficult. If this is the case it is important to ease them gently into being without you. Try leaving them for very short periods of time—only a few minutes if they are really upset by you moving out of sight—and continually come back to reassure them. This will build their confidence and allow you to gradually spend longer periods out of sight, until eventually you can leave them with another adult they trust. It is important, though, to allow your baby however much time *they* need for this stage, as forcing things now can undermine their confidence.

This cycle is completed at their first birthday or solar return. We say 'many happy returns' on birthdays because the Sun returns each year to the same place in the sky as it was at the moment of birth. By this stage your baby has developed their own personality and is developing the confidence to move further afield in their exploration of life.

Baby's first words and thought patterns

'We spend the first year of our children's lives teaching them to walk and talk and the next twelve telling them to sit down and shut up.'
Phyllis Diller

Your child's ability to communicate and absorb information is also linked to their hand/eye coordination. In very young children the early cycles of Mercury represent the development of language and verbal communication.

The first step in the language cycle occurs between eight weeks and four months, when babies begin to smile and gurgle purposefully when making eye contact. This is the first attempt at real communication, as opposed to gurgling for baby's own pleasure. It occurs over quite a wide range of ages and accounts for why some children reach this stage much earlier than others.

The next, and first major, trigger occurs between five and seven months, when baby begins to differentiate sounds, realising they have meaning. This is a whole other step, which coincides with the first opposition of Mercury in your baby's chart. As with all of these developmental stages, the condition of the planet shows the way the skill is developed and integrated. A planet receiving positive aspects such as trines and sextiles integrates much more easily into the personality than one receiving the more difficult square or opposition.

Children with Mercury in an air sign—Aquarius, Gemini and Libra—will be very keen to communicate verbally and usually do so fairly well. Fire signs—Aries, Leo and Sagittarius—can be so keen to get their words out, they actually trip over them, as their mind is working faster than their mouth. Water Mercury signs—Cancer, Scorpio and Pisces—tend to communicate more through their body language and can have some difficulty with words initially, while those with Mercury in earth—Capricorn, Taurus and Virgo—can be very precise and methodical with their communication. Unless they have a major learning difficulty, your baby will eventually start to communicate somewhere between five and seven months.

By between eleven and thirteen and a half months, when Mercury returns to its birth position, your child will be using words with meaning rather than just copying the sounds they hear. They now realise that different sounds have different meanings.

Don't panic if your baby is a late talker; all children go through these stages at differing times. After a few cycles, usually around the third birthday, all children are on a relatively level playing field. Even if you have a child who doesn't seem to 'get it' first time around, they will eventually;

they are following their own timetable. Your child may be like Lancelot Ware, co-founder of Mensa, who had a slow Mercury cycle, as did a more famous Mensa member, Geena Davis.

Becoming social

'If your children spend most of their time in other people's houses, you're lucky; if they all congregate at your house, you're blessed.'
Mignon McLaughlin, **The Second Neurotic's Notebook**, *1966*

As Venus moves around your child's horoscope for the first time, there is a growing awareness of others. Unlike the Sun, which awakens the sense of being separate from others, Venus is related to how we connect to those we meet.

Venus has a very regular orbit and the differences in the age that the different stages occur is solely due to the retrograde cycle and where your child is born in this cycle. A child with a retrograde Venus at birth, or born in the months preceding this period will reach some of these stages later than other children. This can be the shy child who is not as comfortable as their peers in social situations.

The first major stage in becoming social occurs between four and a half months to eight and a half months. During this time your child will begin to show an increasing interest in others, particularly when introduced to their peers. The later this occurs, the more socially aware your child is likely to be.

The first Venus cycle ends at between nine and a half and thirteen and a half months. By this stage you will see whether your child is socially inclined or not. If your child is open and friendly at the completion of the first Venus cycle, this is the way they will be. If they are more self-contained and not overly fussed about others, this is where they are most comfortable. Don't worry if your child is more retiring; not everyone needs an active social life. Some are content with their own company or a few friends. When you understand this aspect of your child's personality it helps you plan play dates, parties and outings your child will enjoy.

The terrible twos

'I love to play hide and seek with my kid, but some days my goal is to find a hiding place where he can't find me until after high school.'

Anonymous

I don't know who wrote that but I have heard many a parent utter something similar when they have a two-year-old in the house.

I remember having a phone conversation with my sister-in-law late one night, when all our children were finally asleep. We decided we should send all the children to boarding school at age two until they were 21. Of course, now it would be more like 30!

The 'terrible twos' are one of the first of the major stages parents are aware of. For most children, this time coincides with the return of the planet Mars to the position it was at the time of birth. This is called the 'Mars return', and it occurs approximately every 22 months. The first Mars return is the most significant for your child, as it is the *first*. This makes perfect sense when you understand Mars is the planet of self-determination, assertion and anger. It gives us the drive and desire to move forward. When Mars returns to its birth position for the first time, it can trigger 'Martian' behaviour in your child. This is why your placid baby suddenly begins to throw temper tantrums: for the first time their little hands become firmly planted on their hips and their favourite word is suddenly 'NO'.

When you understand why these changes are taking place in your child, it is so much easier to deal with. This is the first of many steps your child will take toward their independence. How you handle this first attempt at being their own person will greatly influence how they will attempt independence in the future.

The first Mars return has a major impact on some children, particularly those who have a strong Mars in the birth chart. Mars represents your child's ability to assert themself. It is their drive and momentum, and allows them to take action.

Fostering a child's Mars begins at birth. Babies act initially purely on impulse to external stimulants and their own emotions. There is no processing on a mental level at this point. All of life is a new experience and your baby responds at a basic instinctual, survival level. In the first few months, baby's demands are usually met almost immediately. Baby is fed when hungry, picked up and cuddled when lonely or tired. Eventually a baby begins to connect their actions with the reactions of their carers. If they cry, someone comes to their aid. This is the initial expression of Mars.

As Mars travels on its first cycle in your child's chart, they become more active and more independent. These stages occur at different ages due to the natural cycle of Mars and explain why some children sit, crawl and walk earlier than others. All children receive the energising effect of Mars at different times, and each will respond in their own time.

The first stage of freedom—sitting and crawling

The first Mars stage for babies occurs between *4–11 months* when your baby begins to sit and crawl. Their ability to sit unaided frees their arms and hands and at the same time changes their perspective of the world. See for yourself how different the world looks lying on your back compared to sitting! As their self-determination and dexterity develop, your child is able to consciously make choices by taking or rejecting objects within reach. This ability to independently select and play with objects marks a defining moment because independent movement now becomes an option.

The next step—usually the first step

The second phase occurs between *9–15 months* when your baby begins crawling and walking. Their urge to be independent is now growing. As your child becomes 'upright', they also become a toddler, and the world of self-determination opens. By walking, your toddler realises they can come and go as they choose. This coincides with their first birthday solar return. As children realise they are separate from their parents sometimes they can become overly 'clingy', thinking, *If I can leave, then so can Mum or Dad.* As the toddler becomes increasingly aware of their separateness and their own will, they also reach the next pivotal point in their development: relating to others.

Freedom at last—try keeping up

The third stage is from *13–19 months* and heralds the awakening of greater independence. It is usually where the later walkers come into their own. With increased mobility comes increased freedom and the ability to act on their own behalf. The toddler now develops daring, and with their new-found freedom, they begin to assert their authority. This is when toddlers begin to act out, to prove their autonomy to both themselves and others.

The terrible twos—let the fun begin

The final stage is between *18–24 months* when boundaries are tested fully. As Mars has now completed one full cycle of your child's horoscope, they are now aware they have their own needs and desires. The first Mars return signals the beginning of social awareness and learning to fit in with the needs of others, as well as having our own needs met. Your child can become more demanding and it is of vital importance at this testing time that they understand you are in control. Boundaries become very important now, as do consistent *rules*.

As Mars begins its second journey through your child's chart, they now feel more confident when making demands and being more assertive. That's why some children become aggressive. Mars represents our competitive spirit as well, and is an important factor in our physical and sporting ability. Children generally become more coordinated and much improved at gross motor activities at this time. Activities such as ball games, running and jumping become a source of both pleasure and using up all the Martian energy they are experiencing, and you will notice their skills in these areas are also greatly improved.

If your child is particularly active and difficult during this stage, an introduction to some form of organised physical activity is advisable. This is a good way for them to burn off the excess energy and for you to introduce some discipline in the use of the more assertive/aggressive behaviour. Activities such as kindy gym, swimming lessons and dance would be positive outlets for all this energy.

It is important that your child now feels comfortable expressing their needs and desires, even as they learn what constitutes appropriate expression. It is very important your child knows their needs are heard and acknowledged, and that they begin to differentiate between appropriate and inappropriate ways to speak and behave.

Children who are handled well at this stage are more likely to become proficient at expressing themselves, and more self-reliant. Those who feel ignored, or find that aggression is the best way to get attention, develop negative patterns of behaviour, which won't help you or them. This is the age at which school bullies and their victims are created.

Not all Mars returns are difficult. The child with a fiery Mars may be difficult to handle. On the other hand, a child with a more gentle earth or water placement will become more assertive without the need for temper tantrums.

Two of my sons have Mars in the feminine nurturing sign of Cancer and their first Mars returns were an easy time; they began to take charge of their destiny, without the more negative behaviours. On the other hand, one of my daughters has a very fiery and difficult Mars, she turned into a whirling dervish during her first Mars return, and her 'terrible twos' were about as bad as it gets. She was one of the reasons for the suggestion of a long-term boarding school!

What I didn't do was to give in to her demands, as she needed to learn that there are appropriate and inappropriate ways to express oneself. This isn't easy, but remember: *your child needs you to be a parent, not a 'best friend'*. If you handle these stages well, your child will develop respect for themselves and others.

The terrible twos can be confronting for a parent, particularly if they did not receive appropriate recognition at this stage in their own development. It can be illuminating to look at your reaction to your child's tantrums and demands. Do you feel threatened, angry, or throw your hands up and give in? None of these are a good response. How do you handle stressful situations? Are you able to maintain your perspective, and work through the situation calmly, or do you become the aggressor or the wimp? Your response can indicate how you were treated at the age of two, and give you a clearer understanding of how to best respond to your own child's needs.

School and beyond

'What we want is to see the child in pursuit of knowledge, and not knowledge in pursuit of the child.'
George Bernard Shaw

Education and broadening horizons

Once your child has grasped the basic concepts of language, socialisation and self-assertion it is time to move into the world and expand their horizons. This growth of mind and experience is governed by Jupiter's cycle, which neatly fits in with your child's educational experiences: at the commencement of school, moving into the high school system, and again at the completion of high school and the transition to either further education or work.

As Jupiter is one of the two 'social' planets (the other being Saturn), it means that your child and their friends will experience similar changes at around the same time, unlike the other cycles discussed that are personal and therefore individual. As we have seen, Jupiter also gives your child and their peers a common outlook throughout their education.

With the first major stage in this part of your child's development coinciding with the beginning of their education, where Jupiter is in your child's chart will give much insight into your child's attitude to school. Children with Jupiter in fire signs—Aries, Leo and Sagittarius—will be very keen to experience new things and to learn but may lack concentration. Those with water signs—Pisces, Cancer and Scorpio—need to experience in order to learn. The child with Jupiter in an air sign—Aquarius, Gemini and Libra—will love the social aspect of school and while not finding learning difficult can be ambivalent to the structure of school. Finally, children with Jupiter in an earth sign—Capricorn, Taurus and Virgo—need time to process when they learn. They can also become bogged down with too many facts and figures and learn better experientially, with a hands-on or practical approach.

Referring to Table 3 at the end of the book, showing the major planetary cycles, the later the trigger point—that is, when the planetary contact occurs—the slower your child may be in settling into school and the less comfortable they may be with the whole process. Jupiter opens new possibilities for your child and they will become more outgoing and interested in new subjects and places and more willing to learn at each of these major turning points at around six, twelve and eighteen years. This makes these ages the best time for beginning anything that is related to learning.

Development of responsibility

'The most important thing that parents can teach their children is how to get along without them.'
Frank A. Clark

There are a number of major 'markers' or 'rites of passage' throughout childhood that signify the movement from one level to another. The first comes at seven, when children leave the 'baby' stage behind. Fourteen marks the beginning of puberty and the leaving behind of childhood, while at 21, most western cultures celebrate the reaching of adulthood. All of these ages are linked to the time-keeper, Saturn.

This seven-year growth stage is very tightly linked to the major astrological cycle of Saturn, the planet of responsibility and authority. Saturn, or Chronos, is also known as 'Old Father Time' and the 'Grim Reaper' in reference to his association with maturity and the passage of time.

'A lot of growing up takes place between "It fell" and "I dropped it"'.
Anonymous

The first Saturn square

At around seven years of age, children start to become aware of right and wrong. Before this age a child is not mature enough to completely tell the difference between the truth and a lie, or between fantasy and reality. They are also still developing their visual perception system and depth perception doesn't develop properly until about this age. This is why younger children are unable to cross the road unaided—they don't have the ability to judge speed and distance as an adult does.

Saturn represents responsibility, both personal and collective. It is also about authority figures and boundaries. At the time of the first Saturn square, children may begin to buck against their parents and question things at school. They will also begin to test behavioural boundaries.

This is how they discover how the system works and who has responsibility for what. Ancient wisdom suggests a child is still attached to their mother by an invisible umbilical cord until age seven. It's at seven when most children stop wetting the bed. Some cultures believe children have three spirit guides with them until the age of seven, when they are left with one. In most cultures, seven is considered a magical or spiritual number.

This can be a difficult age for a child and their parents, as the boundaries are constantly stretched, and authority and responsibility questioned. This is a good age to begin giving your child responsibility, but don't expect them to become adults overnight. It is an important milestone, as seven is when the child learns to live within the rules of society, or outside of them. Small responsibilities are the way to go. Allowing children to participate in decision-making about where they go and what they do is a good way to help develop their self-awareness and accountability. This includes sometimes letting them make what may seem the 'wrong' choices. Parents need to lay down clear boundaries with a clear understanding of consequences when children overstep them.

At this age children are also able to take part in the setting of punishments, when the rules are being laid down. Keep to a minimum number of rules, but maintain them firmly. Decide which areas are most important and enforce those areas strictly.

So, if the child asks to play outside and there is a set time to be indoors, discuss the options, then agree on what will happen if they are late coming inside. This way they know the rules and the consequences of breaking those rules. While you may find it difficult, it is extremely important (at this age) to enforce the rules, even if you have to renegotiate them on rare occasions.

This is also a good age for introducing a pet that the child can be responsible for, but realise that the parent will still be the major carer of the animal. The child is learning about responsibility and has a long way to go before mastering it.

'You know your children are growing up when they stop asking you where they came from and refuse to tell you where they're going.'
P.J. O'Rourke

The Saturn opposition

At age fourteen we experience the Saturn opposition, when there is a tendency to see anyone in authority as the enemy. There is a sense of opposing forces, of everyone being against them. This time is usually challenging on a much larger scale than at age seven. Some children become extremely rebellious and confront all forms of authority.

This can particularly affect teenagers with a very strong Saturn energy, or who have a strong Capricorn or Aquarian component in their birth chart.

All children do become more responsible, but generally this will be after a period of rebellion, as they work through the process of creating their own boundaries and personal rules.

'If you want children to keep their feet on the ground, put some responsibility on their shoulders.'
Abigail Van Buren

The second Saturn square

At twenty-one the individual comes of age in many cultures. This is the second Saturn square, but it is now into the waning or closing phase of the cycle. By now an individual has experienced and learnt many things and it is time for them to become responsible for themself. They can no longer blame others for their own mistakes.

The Saturn return

The final phase of this cycle is the Saturn return, between 28 to 30 years of age. Saturn has now completed a full cycle and is back to the starting position, as at the moment of birth. Astrologically this is when an individual is considered to be an adult, as they have experienced a full cycle of learning. By now Saturn has made contact with every planet in your chart, which has touched every facet of your being.

At this age many people will feel an urgency to settle down and become responsible. Many will get married or have their first child at around this age. It is a time of looking back and questioning, then deciding one's future path. This is why many feel concern at turning 30. There is the recognition deep within our soul that this is a major turning point in our lives. For most this will involve a moving on or change of direction in some form. And so the cycle begins again.

Rebel or individual?

'Children in a family are like flowers in a bouquet: there's always one determined to face in an opposite direction from the way the arranger desires.'

Marcelene Cox

The last major cycle affecting childhood is that of the planet Uranus. This planet is representative of the individual and when the first contact occurs at around ten years, your child will begin to show their unique self. This is not a rebellious time but one when your child will want to choose their own clothing and may decide they don't want to do the 'family' thing all the time. They will look for more time alone, and to do the things they are interested in.

It is important that as parents you support your children in their choices and allow them to express themselves in a safe manner. My children were allowed to choose their own clothing and hairstyles, once they were ready. I felt that if I allowed them to express themselves in this way, it might help to prevent rebellion and other less positive shows of independence later on. One of my sons only wore clothing that was several sizes too big and had the most bizarre haircuts, but he was happy. Now he's a young adult in management with a short-back-and-sides haircut, and he wears a shirt and tie to work every day. He is comfortable with who he is, can be himself, but still take on a 'role' in society.

Your child may prefer to wear one colour or multi colours. They may decide they don't really want to learn the piano, or take ballet lessons or that they do. Whatever their preferences, it helps to know that when Uranus becomes active, so will your child's desire to be an individual.

Aries child

Ruling Planet—Mars ♂
Element—Fire
Quality—Cardinal
Sign—the Ram
Glyph—♈
Gemstone—Diamond
Metal—Iron
20 March–19 April

'If your child is to keep their inborn sense of
wonder, they need the companionship of at least
one adult who can share it, rediscovering with
them the joy, excitement and mystery of the world
we live in.'

Rachel Carson

Aries is an action-oriented sign, full of fire and energy. So if your child is born under this sign, they will tend to be active, involved and concerned with the here and now. An Aries child likes instant gratification and has difficulty with the concept of patience. As the parent of an Aries child you will realise very quickly that your child wants their needs met immediately, and will loudly let you know if you aren't responding quickly enough. One of the greatest lessons for your child, and the one that will test you most as a parent, is patience.

There's a saying among astrologers that you can always pick the person with a strong Aries (Mars energy) by the scars on their head or face. Very few Aries children leave childhood without at least one 'battle scar', due to their enthusiasm and tendency to be daredevils.

Each of the twelve zodiac signs has a 'ruling' planet that is the major influence, more so than the sign itself. Mars is the ruling planet affecting Aries. How it is placed in the birth horoscope will be the major influence on your child's personality and this explains why all Aries children are not the same. For example, the Aries child with Mars in Pisces, Cancer and Scorpio will be much more sensitive than the 'average' Aries, Mars in Gemini, Libra and Aquarius will tend to be more of a chatterbox, Mars in Capricorn, Taurus and Virgo will be more grounded and directed while Mars in Aries, Leo and Sagittarius will be constantly active.

Mars is also associated with the day Tuesday, and the number nine, so your Aries child may find them lucky.

your child's will

You will notice fairly quickly that your darling little Aries can be demanding, vocal and loud. They seek immediate satisfaction and may not respond well to an enforced routine. They want what they want NOW! At the same time they can be absolutely delightful and very friendly. Your Aries child will be for the most part a happy child. They have the most delightful grins that just light up the room and all those in it.

Be prepared: your little Aries will be alert and very active and tend to sleep in short bursts rather than for long periods. They are likely to wake easily so it would be a good idea to get them used to sleeping with normal levels of noise and activity going on around them. Leave a radio going in their room when they are sleeping, and do the normal things you need to do, rather than creeping around whispering while they are asleep. You will be doing everyone a favour in the long run.

your Aries baby
from birth to 6 months

- Demanding, vocal and loud
- Alert and active
- Tends to sleep in short bursts and wakes easily
- May become distressed easily but is just as quickly pacified
- Likes physical contact and interaction
- Doesn't like schedule and routine

- Stimulated more by sight than by sound
- Doesn't like restrictive clothing or bedding

Needs time alone with parents, quick response, affection, supervision and freedom to be active

Doesn't like being left alone

your Aries baby

Your Aries baby will display their eagerness almost from the moment they are born. You have a baby who is not content to wait for anything. You may have difficulty if trying to implement a regular schedule with your Aries baby, as they are spontaneous and don't fit well into a routine. This doesn't mean that you shouldn't persist. Your baby does need to fit in with the household routine, but be mindful that it may not be easy.

Your baby will be happy and outgoing but can be demanding. Their need for speed means that they tend to sleep in short bursts and they will tend to settle into a better sleep pattern once they are more active. Your child will be likely to reach their early developmental milestones ahead of time, as they are eager to become independent and on the move. When your baby becomes unsettled, the best way to soothe them is through movement, either by rocking as you walk, taking them for a walk in the pram or a drive in the car.

your Aries baby
from 6 to 18 months

- Very active
- May try to walk before learning to crawl
- Impatient—as much with themself as others
- Becomes frustrated if they can't achieve things as quickly as they would like
- Likely to be an early walker
- Into everything and everywhere
- Learns through experience

Needs supervision, safe areas to explore, mild restriction, early lessons in patience and waiting

Doesn't like restraint, getting hurt, isolation and especially being ignored

your Aries toddler

Your Aries toddler may become distressed and even angry easily, but is just as quickly pacified. They are easily distracted by anything new, and while this may have a downside, the upside is that when they do become upset they are fairly easily diverted from the source of distress and towards something else.

Your Aries toddler will be interested in whatever is going on around them, want to be a part of everything, at least briefly, and won't enjoy missing out on anything. They will benefit from interactive and action games, such as pat-a-cake or row the boat.

Your Aries child is likely to be more physical than many other children, and will keep you on the go. They may oppose too much schedule and routine, preferring life to happen spontaneously and will be outgoing, enjoying their interaction with others.

You will find your child responds better to visual cues than auditory ones, and will be stimulated by sight more than sound. So make sure you have a good supply of bright picture books to read together, and spend time drawing and painting, and taking in the details around you when you're outside.

Your toddler will not like restrictive clothing or bedding, so you may have difficulty keeping covers on them. During winter an all-in-one sleep suit would be better than two-piece pyjamas, so even if they kick off their blankets they will still have some cover for warmth. One young Aries child I know felt so restricted by clothing that she would regularly greet visitors dressed only in her birthday suit. Her parents tried to keep clothing on her, to no avail until she moved out of this phase and into school. Until then they let her wear her swimsuit, which at least she would keep on.

As they grow they will become increasingly more active and may try to walk before learning to crawl. Your child will also grow ever more impatient—as much with themself as others. This child can become frustrated if they can't achieve things at least by their second attempt.

It is advisable to introduce them to early lessons in patience, waiting and tolerance. Don't keep them waiting for too long initially, as this may create the opposite result. As they get older you can have them count out the time they have to wait. Start by having them count to ten, and then gradually increase the waiting time. This will not only help them to develop patience, it also helps them to understand the concept of time and, of course, develops and improves their number skills.

They are likely to be early walkers, adventurous and be into everything. Remember, your child learns through experience and therefore needs to explore and expand their horizons to gain this experience. They need supervision and safe areas to explore, along with boundaries, to keep them secure.

Once your little Aries is able to walk, they will also become argumentative and even a little rebellious, questioning authority. At this stage also, they will begin experimenting with testing the boundaries. Parents may find this a difficult phase as your Aries child now questions and argues your every decision, and constantly stretches the limits. Don't be alarmed; they are trying to sort out who is who in the family and where they fit in the scheme of things. They will go through this phase many times as they grow. If you can remember why, it may make things a little easier for you both. Treat their questions and challenges fairly and calmly, and life together will move along much more quickly and smoothly.

Toilet training

This can become a battleground, if you allow it to. There may be an expectation this little one will grasp toileting as quickly and easily as they have crawling, walking and talking. The reality is that they may be so busy doing other things that remembering to go to the toilet may not be a high priority. Your little Aries will begin to use the toilet when they are ready and not one minute before. Cajoling and making it an issue is only likely to lengthen the process. Allow your child to guide you in this matter. Be supportive and encouraging, but try not to take control.

your Aries toddler from 18 months to 3 years

- Increasingly inquisitive
- Drives adults to distraction with endless questions
- Always busy
- Constantly on the move
- Becoming argumentative and even a little rebellious
- Will question authority
- Begins experimenting with testing the boundaries
- Continues to be active, can be accident-prone

Needs a safe environment in which to explore, to be able to argue and question, continual lessons in patience—including self-patience, firmer limits, supervision, and support

Doesn't like being ignored, humiliated, condescension, lack of boundaries, and lack of protection

your child's emotions

The Moon in a birth chart represents your child's emotions and instinctual responses. It is an excellent indicator of how they respond in emotional situations. The Moon rules infancy and early childhood, and is the face of your child that you will see most often during the early years.

Emotions are also associated with the element water, as is the Moon. As the Moon waxes and wanes, we see the effects on the tides. It also affects all living beings. The Moon is instinctive, intuitive and empathetic. The Moon reflects the light from the Sun and is associated with similar attributes for your child. The Moon shows how your child deals with mood changes and emotions, and how your child learns to become reflective and store memories.

If you have an Aries Moon child, they have a Moon with 'attitude'. When the Moon is in Aries, it will certainly add fire to your child's personality. They may be quite demanding when young. They may also run hot and cold emotionally. Some days they can't seem to get enough cuddles, and other days they don't want you to touch them.

Your child will be independent and may become quite annoyed if you 'interfere' while they are trying to master something new. They will be happy for you to show them how to do something once, but after that, expect the response 'I can do it myself' if you should offer any further assistance.

Like their animal counterpart, the ram, Aries tend to go into situations headfirst and for this reason the head and face are the most vulnerable parts of the body for your Aries child. They can also be prone to headaches, especially when under emotional stress.

Full speed ahead is the way your child will tackle most things in life. They will not be one to linger over meals. 'Get it over and done with as quickly as possible, so I can move onto something else', will be their attitude. They will rush from one thing to another, leaving a trail of half-finished projects in their wake. Your Aries child will need to learn perseverance and patience. Neither of them will be easy lessons for any of you.

Aries children resonate to the colour red and it is indicative of their nature: a little like the red fire engine on the way to a fire. Red is the colour of assertiveness but for the little Aries too much red can send them over the top. A touch of calming green or blue added to their colour scheme can help soothe.

your Aries preschooler

By preschool age, your Aries child doesn't like being ignored or humiliated and may feel insecure if there is a lack of boundaries or lack of protection. So even though they may push against both, your little Aries needs to know they are there.

The cheerful Aries baby and toddler can become quite a volatile preschooler and needs firm limits about what is and isn't acceptable when asserting themselves. As a youngster, your Aries child may have difficulty in distinguishing between assertion, independence and aggression. Aries children need to develop courage, initiative and independence, hence they are unlikely to fall in with the group as much as be the leader.

Aries enjoy strong-tasting foods such as onion and garlic and you may find it useful to include small amounts of these foods in their diet once their palate is mature enough to appreciate them.

They are also likely to be extremely sensitive and can take everything personally while they are going through these stages. They can be impatient and won't care to wait for anything. Part of the Aries nature is to move, not to stand still. Your Aries child may also become increasingly frustrated at their inability to perform certain tasks that may be beyond their preschool capacity.

Another skill that they will need help with from the time they are very young, is persevering and not losing interest. Perhaps setting small tasks and small portions of time spent attending to one thing would be a good way to encourage your child to apply themself to something for longer periods of time. As they get older the time spent can be increased, slowly lengthening their attention span. Although they need clear explanations, they will bristle at being lectured.

At this age, they still require ample physical activity, and five or six is a good age to introduce them to organised and team sports. They may not be a particularly sporty child but will be competitive in whatever they do, even if only competing against their self-imposed standards. The chances are that your child will be rather physical. Little athletics, martial arts or dance classes can be good for coordination and burning off excess energy. Children born under the sign of Aries seem to have batteries that never run low. It is good to encourage them to take time-out periods to help them learn to relax, and prevent burnout when they are older. Learning to use energy constructively and conservatively is an extremely valuable lesson.

Aries, being the first of the signs, is very direct. It's important to understand that your child expects honest answers, rather than evasive explanations. They will most need your guidance when learning patience, and being taught to take quiet time and to be assertive without being overly aggressive.

Aries children are delightful, gregarious and exuberant little people who will bring much warmth and happiness into your life.

your Aries preschooler
from 3 to 6 years

- Rapid emotional responses
- Can be extremely sensitive, taking everything personally
- Likes to get on with things
- Frustrated at inability to perform certain tasks
- Developing comparative skills: bigger, smallest, first, last, etc.
- Requires honest explanation but not lectures
- Attention span still short
- Requires physical activity, good age to introduce to organised and team sports
- Beginning to grasp the concept of consequences of actions

Needs honesty, protection, information, explanations, assistance with developing patience and an understanding of consequences of actions

Doesn't like lectures, labels, rejection, humiliation, restriction, boredom and waiting

Fun, friendship and confidence

Your Aries will be warm and outgoing, and have no problem making friends as they get older. Keeping them may be a little harder, as Aries will be as demanding of their friends as they are on you. Your child is a born initiator; they like to lead the way and can't understand why others aren't moving at the same speed. Life has so much to sample, and they want to try it all.

Your child will be a real little daredevil, with very little sense of danger; they have a genuine need for excitement in their life. Any form of physical activity will help them to burn off some of their excess emotional energy and they will be much more of an outdoors child than indoors.

Your Aries child can learn quite quickly and without too much trouble, but concentrating on one thing for any length of time can be difficult. They may learn to read quite early, but don't expect them to sit still for too long and read a book. Even your little Aries girl would much rather be outside climbing a tree. This is where it can be difficult for Aries when school begins. They would prefer to be out in the playground than stuck in the classroom. They have boundless energy. If you can help them to harness this enthusiasm, they can move mountains.

Your Aries child can be prone to temper tantrums if they don't get their own way and will need to learn to control angry outbursts. They may be quick to anger, but just as quick to cool down. Once they have expressed their anger or disappointment, the incident is quickly forgotten. This is not a child to hold a grudge or sulk over anything.

To keep them happy, keep them moving. Long walks outside, either in their pram, or when they are a little older with them running along beside you, will help to settle them. Massage can help quieten them, and also help them learn to relax a little. Their biggest lesson will be learning to slow down and enjoy all that life has to offer.

Aries children don't understand the word 'can't' and, like their symbol, the ram, will meet all obstacles head down and forward.

First impressions

The ascendant, or rising sign in your child's horoscope is where heaven meets Earth: the part of the sky that is visible on the horizon, looking directly to the east at the time of birth. Some say this represents the soul's entry into the earthly plane. In a birth chart it represents the physical body of an individual and shows how we meet the world head-on. It is referred to as the mask we wear when we first meet people, the filter through which all of the planets within the birth horoscope are expressed.

Your child is likely to have made quite an entrance into the world. Aries is ruled by the planet Mars, and there is nothing slow or subtle where Mars is concerned; this is the planet of action and energy. With an Aries ascendant, your child will have a personality that is positive, aggressive, competitive and in perpetual motion. Mars can also add a touch of red to the colouring, particularly the hair. An Aries ascendant will not necessarily give your child a crop of red hair, but it could well add a touch of colour or highlights to their natural colour.

Your child is full of enthusiasm and expectation. They will have a tendency to become bored easily and can be impatient if things don't happen as quickly as they would like. With a short attention span they will need a variety of toys to keep them occupied.

Your Aries child will be very physical and active. Aries on the ascendant can give a combination of above-average sporting ability, combined with a strong competitive spirit. If they can learn to control their strong will, they will be capable of achieving anything they set their mind to. There is a strong tendency to be impulsive and to act before thinking. This can lead to falls and accidents. Your child will have no hesitation about jumping in where angels fear to tread, and they may suffer the consequences. They are physically keen and alert, with quick reflexes.

Your child will be very assertive and you can expect many battles as they grow and test their strong will.

your Aries child from 7 to 10 years

This is the beginning of the development of responsibility. Aries has a tendency to rush whatever they do and this can be a positive time in learning to do something well, rather than quickly. Provide your child with small tasks initially that they can complete without becoming bored and provide a suitable reward scheme. A daily star chart, which has a larger reward when a certain number of stars is reached, can be ideal. It will teach your impatient Aries child to set goals and slowly work towards them.

Introduce your child to the democracy of setting rules and the consequences for breaking those rules. Rule-setting should preferably be discussed together as a family and definitely before wrongdoing occurs. Don't expect your child to grasp these concepts quickly, as even though the Aries nature is quick-thinking, where responsibility is concerned, learning can be a long, slow process.

> As Aries children come under the influence of the planet Mars, the cell salt that is most of use to them in times of stress is Kali Phos (potassium phosphate). It helps rebalance the system and can be particularly useful during puberty.

your Aries teen from 11 to 14 years

As the teenager emerges, life can become interesting in the Aries household. While being an Aries does not make the child more rebellious than any other, these developing young adults are usually more assertive than their peers born under other signs. As with all other stages in this child's development, boundaries remain important. Remember that when your child begins to challenge authority it means they are ready to take on more responsibility for themself. It is vitally important, though, that your child learns at this point that assertiveness is not the same as aggressiveness.

Your Aries teen has plenty of enthusiasm in starting something new but lacks the tenacity to see things to completion, so this is also a time when you can help them develop the skill of perseverance, which is just as important as tackling a new task with enthusiasm. It is still important that you allow the emerging adult to take part in rule-making and the setting of appropriate punishments when rules are broken.

Aries are talented at any number of professions, as the list of famous Aries shows. They have an aptitude for the performing arts, and figure prominently among composers: J.S. Bach, Stephen Sondheim and Andrew Lloyd Webber are just a few examples. They need a career that involves excitement and variety; they will stagnate in a regular nine-to-five type career path, unless they have a strong earth component elsewhere in their horoscope. They are also well suited to a career that keeps them active, such as with the Fire or Police service. Primary school teacher, farmer or chemist are other suitable career choices. Your child will be creative and dynamic and needs a career choice that reflects that and allows them the freedom to make decisions and be heard. Your child may also find themself gravitating to a more altruistic profession where they feel they are of some assistance to others in their community such as working for a charity.

The young Aries adult

This young person is likely to be so busy with their fingers in so many pies that you hardly ever see them! Aries doesn't like to sit still for too long, and as the young adult emerges they continue to sample various activities and lifestyles. This can be a testing time that usually involves a clash of wills. These young adults will be keen to take total responsibility as soon as possible, although they will still enjoy the home comforts and having things done for them. Taking care of the little things in life, such as doing their own washing, may not be part of their idea of independence and they will also have some wonderful excuse as to why. Truth is, for these young adults, life offers so much to be experienced and they don't want to waste a moment on doing trivial things.

It is important that you, as their parent, don't fall into the trap of taking on jobs they should be doing. You have nurtured and encouraged their independence and responsibility up to this point. Be firm and persistent: remind your young adult that independence and personal responsibility go hand in hand. No matter the arguments that result, it is important that you continue now. They are still not quite ready to take on the world until they can at least take care of their own laundry!

Although not necessarily prickly themselves, throughout history Aries has been assigned to all thorn-bearing trees, and honeysuckle, thistle, bryony, hawthorn, spruce. Growing these in the garden or even a picture on the bedroom or playroom wall can be of benefit to your Aries child.

Famous Aries

Marlon Brando
Charlie Chaplin
Joan Crawford
Andrew Lloyd Webber
Stephen Sondheim
Raphael
Johann Sebastian Bach
Bela Bartok
Franz Joseph Haydn
Eric Clapton
Celine Dion
Modest Mussorgsky
Thomas Jefferson
Joseph Pulitzer
Nikita Khrushchev
Vincent Van Gogh
Jack Brabham
Wilbur Wright
Robert Helpmann
Brett Whiteley
Hugh Hefner

Russell Crowe
Reese Witherspoon
Claire Danes
Kate Hudson
Sarah Jessica Parker
Elle Macpherson
William Shatner
Judy Nunn
Victoria Beckham
Eddie Murphy
Keira Knightley
Mandy Moore
Fergie (singer)
Mariah Carey
Elton John
David Tennant
Emma Watson
Robbie Coltrane
Casanova
Francis Ford Coppola
Colin Powell

Taurus child

Ruling Planet—Venus ♀
Element—Earth
Quality—Fixed
Sign—the Bull
Glyph—♉
Gemstone—Emerald
Metal—Copper
19 April–20 May

'There are two lasting bequests we can give our children. One is roots. The other is wings.'

Henry Ward Beecher

Children born under the sign of Taurus are loyal, steadfast, determined, and sensual. By sensual I mean they take in their environment through the integration of all of the senses. They love to eat, sleep and enjoy physical contact. One thing is for certain: they will appreciate all of the good things that life has to offer. Taureans are for the most part of a gentle nature, but can be extremely stubborn and will stand their ground when their mind is set.

One of the first things that you will notice with your Taurus child is how placid they are. They are probably one of the easiest of the twelve Sun signs as babies and young children. They are easy to please and love lots of cuddles, settling best if they are swaddled (wrapped tightly), as they enjoy being close and snug. Taurus babies do better with demand feeding in preference to an imposed schedule initially, but will quickly settle into their own pattern.

Venus is the ruling planet affecting Taurus. How it is placed in the birth horoscope will be the major influence on your child's personality and this explains why all Taurus children are not the same. The Taurus child with Venus in Aries will be a more dynamic and forceful child than the 'average' Taurus, Venus in Taurus adds to the sensual qualities, while Venus in Gemini will tend to be more of a chatterbox. Venus in Cancer or Pisces adds sensitivity and creativity, as well as making your child more intuitive. (Venus can never be further than two signs away from the Sun, so these are the only possible positions of this planet for the Taurus child.)

Venus is associated with the day Friday and the number six, so your Taurus child may find them lucky.

your child's will

Although Taurus may appear to be a little slower than other children of the same age, don't confuse speed with intelligence. It takes longer to assimilate their environment through all five senses. Realise from the outset that your Taurus child doesn't like to be rushed. They need time to absorb new things and appreciate what they are doing now, before moving on to the next thing.

Your child needs plenty of reassurance to help build their confidence. The security of routine will also become increasingly important as they grow. When this routine is interrupted, changed or challenged in any way, then you will see the real bull stand their ground. As they grow, their determination and stubbornness continue to develop. Your child can really become the immovable object once their mind is made up over something, or if they're feeling undue stress. Rather than meet this head-on, try diversion. Calm the situation first, and allow some 'cool down' time before gently dismantling their mood or obsession. Bribery can work a treat with your Taurus child but whatever you do, don't allow this to become a habit. Save it for extreme circumstances and always as a point of compromise.

your Taurus baby
from birth to 6 months

- Loves cuddles
- Prefers to be swaddled
- Very sensitive to physical discomfort

- Good feeder but prefers close physical contact during feeding
- Does better with demand feeding in preference to a schedule
- Needs physical closeness for reassurance
- Will not respond well to change in their schedule from outside influences
- If they are unsettled, check the physical comforts first

Needs physical contact and to have basic needs met promptly

Doesn't like being hungry or overtired

your Taurus baby

The young Taurus is an undemanding and easy baby. There are a few very simple things this baby needs to be content. Food, sleep and security are top on the list. If these things are taken care of, you will have a happy baby. In fact, one of the biggest problems with your Taurus baby will be their tendency to sleep so well you may have to wake them for their feeds. You should find this little one begins to sleep through the night quite early. If the longer sleep cycle is during the day it is a relatively simple process to gradually move it to the night.

Remember, if they become unsettled, always check the physical comforts first. Is baby hungry or wet or just needs the reassurance of a cuddle? They will usually be very easy to settle if these things are taken care of. Massage is an excellent way of satisfying their need for touch as well as helping with bonding and being very relaxing. Both you and your baby will benefit from attending a baby massage class.

your Taurus baby
from 6 to 18 months

- Enjoys discovering things using all of their senses
- Tends to 'mouth' everything they come into contact with
- Toys that allow a lot of tactile exploration and stimulus are best
- Likely to develop an attachment to a 'special' cuddly toy—security blanket style
- May appear to be a little slower than other children of the same age
- Doesn't like to be rushed, and will react negatively to being pushed

Needs time to assimilate and learn new things, reassurance, physical contact

Doesn't like rushing, hunger, discomfort or feeling unsafe

your Taurus toddler

As a toddler, your child may be anywhere from passively resistant to, in extreme cases, an outright tantrum-thrower. They will still respond best to a gentle and loving touch rather than a talking to, or especially bullying.

Explanations of new concepts need to be accompanied by graphic examples with as much detail as possible. Remember, they learn best when able to integrate multiple senses and they need time to do this. Your Taurus toddler doesn't like surprise or unexpected events. It is best to give them plenty of time to adjust to major changes, particularly if a change threatens their feeling of security.

They need plenty of 'hands on' experience when learning something new. It is not enough to just show them or give an explanation: they need to 'do' what they are being taught. They will enjoy working alongside you in the garden or the kitchen and will love to feel and smell the things they are working with. These are ideal environments for your toddler as there is so much sensory experience in both of these places.

Your child will need your help to learn about give and take, and being assertive. Their own strong will can sometimes get in the way of their ability to compromise. They may be so determined that they can be seen as pushy. Toddlers need to learn to temper this attribute and use it in a more appropriate way so that they are not walked over by others, but neither do they constantly bulldoze their way ahead.

Your toddler's early explorations and discovery will involve all of their senses. They tend to 'mouth' everything they come into contact with. Taurus is the most sensuous of all signs and your Taurus child will want to explore how things smell, taste and feel, instead of simply how they look or sound.

Toys that allow tactile exploration and stimulus are best for your child. They will enjoy the soft feel of a teddy bear, or the scent of their freshly washed bed clothes. They are likely to develop an attachment to a 'special' cuddly toy at some stage during their early years and there may be difficulty getting them to sleep if the favourite toy is missing for any reason.

They will enjoy music, art, theatre and all of the other finer things in life. Music can be particularly useful when they are very small. Gentle music playing in the background can be very beneficial in helping to settle your Taurus child when fractious. As they get a little older they will amuse themself with song and will delight you at the same time with their sweet, melodious voice.

Your child will respond well to sounds and you can use music as a cue to the events of the day. A different song for dinnertime, bathtime and bedtime, for example, can work very well with your child.

You will find your Taurus toddler will tend to stay fairly close and is not generally prone to wandering too far in their explorations. This is where it becomes important to gradually develop their self-confidence, so they feel comfortable enough to remove their grip from around your leg in the first instance and slowly extend their boundaries. Remember to do this with gentle encouragement and not force.

Toilet training

Toilet training can be either very easy or a bone of contention and drag on forever. Remember to be patient and not hurry your little Taurean; allow them to do this in their own time. A reward system can help things move along swiftly. If you allow their own determination to kick in, they will achieve results very quickly. If on the other hand you try to put pressure on them and hurry them along, the Taurean stubbornness will kick back, and this will very quickly become the source of a power struggle—which in the end no one wins.

your Taurus toddler
from 18 months to 3 years

- Determination and stubbornness begin to really show
- Needs plenty of forewarning of any changes

- May be anywhere from passively resistant to, in extreme cases, outright tantrum-throwers
- Still responds best to a gentle and loving touch rather than talk
- Explanations of new concepts need to be accompanied by graphic examples with plenty of detail

Needs plenty of 'hands on' experience; to begin learning about compromise and being assertive

Doesn't like surprise and unexpected happenings, being forced, rushed, embarrassed or put down, lack of attention, being neglected or going hungry

your child's emotions

The Moon in a birth chart represents your child's emotions and instinctual responses. It is an excellent clue to how they respond in emotional situations. The Moon rules infancy and early childhood, and is the face of your child that you will see most often during the early years.

Emotions are also associated with the element water, as is the Moon. As the Moon waxes and wanes, we see the effects on the tides. It also affects all living beings as we also wax and wane. The Moon is instinctive, intuitive, reflective and empathetic. The Moon reflects the light from the Sun and is associated with similar attributes for your child. The Moon in a birth chart represents your child's emotions and instinctual responses. Your child's emotions can be closely tied to the food they eat. The texture and smell of the food you prepare for your child can be just as important as the taste. Your scent can be as important a clue to who you are as your touch, and both will be more important to your child than the way you look. It is important not to overwork your child's senses with too much variety when they are very tiny. Try to keep artificial scents to a minimum until they get a little older; they would much prefer to be able to recognise a clean, natural smell.

Your Taurus child will find their greatest comfort from being snuggled tightly by you. They need physical contact more than just about any other sign. If your child becomes fractious and hard to settle, try using gentle massage to help them relax and to calm. Using a mix of a few drops of lavender and chamomile oils in a gentle carrier oil can do wonders for soothing your Taurus child, no matter their age. Rub the massage oil gently over their torso, working in gentle circular strokes over the tummy area and up and down over the rest of the body. This is a total sensual experience for your child and one that both they and you will enjoy greatly, especially when you see the tension gradually easing from their little body. It is best to leave bath until the last thing before bed, especially if you find your child becoming distressed around this time regularly. This way, you can follow the bath with the gentle massage routine, and bedtime and, more importantly, sleep. This becomes the natural and easy progression.

The throat is the most vulnerable part of the body for your Taurus child and they can be prone to tonsillitis and ear and throat infections, especially when under emotional stress.

Your child will enjoy being carried around as you go about your daily chores and is an ideal baby for a baby sling. You will find they will sleep quite contentedly as you vacuum, clean or even mow the lawn, snuggled in against your chest. Don't worry that they won't eventually settle into sleeping in a bed as they get a little older, as the only thing they will enjoy more than their food is a comfortable bed.

Once they are asleep, they will sleep through just about anything. The only problem you may have in this area is colic, as they enjoy their food so much, they may have a tendency to feed a little too quickly at first and this can lead to problems. If breastfeeding, try giving the first feed of the morning lying on your back, as they will have to work a little harder to get their milk and it won't flow quite so quickly. If bottle-feeding, use a slow-flow teat for the first feed of the morning. Providing you can get the first feed of the day right, it should eliminate that dreadful colic time late in the afternoon. If they still have a problem, a warm bath with a few drops of lavender oil and gentle massage of the tummy should help. The good news here is that colic usually settles after about six weeks.

They will have a healthy appetite and when they get a little older will follow you around the kitchen as you prepare their meals, savouring the smells and waiting impatiently for their dinner to be ready. They will enjoy helping you to prepare food as they also like the feel of the food. They may choose to use their fingers to feed, long after they should be using cutlery. This is because they take pleasure in the sensation of food on their fingers almost as much as when it is in their mouth.

Taurus children resonate to the colours green and brown. They like their lives to be calm and predictable and these earthy colours represent that. Pastel shades are also a soothing backdrop for them. Even dressing them in these colours (especially during times of stress), can be very therapeutic. Conversely, use more vibrant colours, such as reds and orange, when you feel they need a boost of energy or courage.

your Taurus preschooler

By preschool age, your placid little Taurean is now beginning to develop new behaviour patterns that may temporarily throw parents. The Taurus preschooler can become quite competitive and this can show up as sibling rivalry, generally over possessions. Patience and perseverance will become valuable tools for parents during this time.

Taurus is very concerned with possession and needs to know what belongs to whom. They will not take kindly to others taking what is theirs and may need help with the concept of sharing. It is important that they are also shown respect and that their 'special' things should be a 'no go' area, unless they choose to share them.

Your Taurus child's preferred foods include cereals, berry fruits, apples, pears, asparagus and most fragrant spices (not hot).

Your child can become more assertive as a preschooler. They are very concerned with getting their fair share and will begin to notice any anomalies. This is part of the ongoing discovery of who they are. Your Taurus child needs firm guidelines on acceptable limits to assertiveness, but as they have a tendency to be non-assertive, it is also important not to completely stifle this area of their development.

Your Taurus child may also become increasingly frustrated if they are unable to perform certain tasks. Remember, they need time to master new skills, so encourage them to persevere. This is another skill your child will need help with from the time they are very young. Encourage them to take breaks if they become frustrated and resume what they are trying to master after they have had some time out doing something they are confident with.

School can be a challenge as they will now have to face time pressures. Things have to be done within a certain time and they may have difficulty at first in completing work on time. They will enjoy the social interaction and the routine of school. Encourage them as much as possible in the early years, giving plenty of support and assistance. Remember, their need to move slowly does not mean they are 'slow'. Many a parent *and* teacher of a little Taurean has had a pleasant surprise when the end-of-year exams come around and they are able to show just how much they really have learnt during the year. As they get older, lessons in time management would be a good idea.

your Taurus preschooler from 3 to 6 years

● May now be less easy to please than they were previously

- More active and instigative
- Becoming competitive
- May appear more selfish and less happy

Needs explanations, advance warning of changes, experience, information, reassurance, encouragement, rewards, affection (verbal now as well as tactile), continued lessons in compromise, extra support while learning to accept change

Doesn't like pressure, rushing, being out of control, unpredictability, change, rejection or ridicule

Fun, friendship and confidence

Your little Taurus will tend to have a small group of close friends that they will keep throughout school and into adulthood. Your child will enjoy mixing with others but will tend to be fairly conservative in most choices in life.

With the need for sensual satisfaction that all Taureans share, your child will gain much pleasure from being involved in the arts. Music, art and dance will have a strong attraction for your child. They will particularly enjoy music and may like to join a musical society, choir or orchestra when old enough. Equally, they will gain much pleasure from observing the creativity of others. Trips to the art gallery, concerts and ballet may be things they will benefit from when older.

Your Taurus child may be a little hesitant initially, as they take their time assessing any new situation. With increasing confidence they will spread their wings and fly, and in doing so broaden their horizons.

Your child will enjoy the pleasures that life has to offer and this is one child who has an inborn sense of knowing how to stop and smell the roses, or sit and admire the beauty of a sunset. Do yourself a favour occasionally and join your child in their world. It is one of beauty and calm.

The animal most associated with Taurus is the bull and other cattle. This animal represents the steadfastness of the Taurus characteristics. Like their animal counterpart, Taureans tend to be slow to get moving but once they get going are almost unstoppable.

First impressions

The ascendant, or rising sign in your child's horoscope is where heaven meets Earth: the part of the sky that is visible on the horizon, looking directly to the east at the time of birth. Some say this represents the soul's entry into the earthly plane. In a birth chart it represents the physical body of an individual and shows how we meet the world head-on. It is referred to as the mask we wear when we first meet people, the filter through which all of the planets within the birth horoscope are expressed.

With Taurus on the ascendant, your child has a stable, graceful and harmonious personality. They will be affectionate, and steadfastly loyal to those they love. Their needs are fairly simple: good food, a warm comfy bed and pleasant surroundings. They will be for the most part passive in nature and easygoing until they are pushed. When they are provoked they can become extremely stubborn and display a raging bull temper. Fortunately this doesn't happen very often, as it takes a lot for this child to lose control.

Your child will tend to be reserved and not likely to take chances. They will stop and think of the consequences before taking any action. They can be very selfish of both their possessions and people who are close to them. Although they can be a little slow to get motivated, once they begin something they will see it through until the end, no matter how long it takes.

As Taurus governs the area of the neck and throat this little one may have more than their fair share of sore throats and perhaps even tonsillitis. Your child may have a very pleasant speaking and even singing voice, as can be seen in the list of famous Taureans. There may be a tendency toward being a little heavy, but they will have strength and endurance.

Your Taurus child will be dependable when it comes to carrying out tasks that you have set for them, but don't expect anything to be done quickly. They will do things at their own pace and in their own time and nothing and no one can speed them up. Left to work within their own time frame and with your encouragement, they will always reach their target in the end.

Your Taurus child's tactile senses will continue to be a source of pleasure as they grow and they will be drawn to the more 'luxurious' things in life: the sensual satisfaction that they can only get from natural fibres such as real cotton, wool, silk, leather, and so on. These children draw on all senses for experience; the smell and feel is as important as taste and look.

your Taurus child
from 7 to 10 years

The Taurus child, by this age, is normally quite consistent when it comes to dependability and works well within a routine. This time is usually a positive stage for them, especially when handled well. They still need time to complete tasks so try to set fairly simple challenges at first and allow your child enough time to complete them. It is important not to rush your developing Taurus, as this will only lead to a sense of frustration, when what they need now is a developing sense of achievement.

Your child needs to be given more responsibility at this stage but Taurus does have a tendency to plod along, which can be frustrating for the parent. Perhaps you could use a star chart based on the time it takes to complete a task, with a new star gained every time they beat their own record. This will encourage them to be responsible and at the same time help them learn to move at a slightly faster pace.

Taurus children come under the influence of the planet Venus and for them the most beneficial of the cell salts is Nat Sulph (sodium sulphate). This can be useful during times of stress or as a general tonic when they are lacking in energy.

your Taurus teen
from 11 to 14 years

As the teenager emerges, your Taurus child can become even more stubborn. This same stubbornness, when harnessed, becomes determination. Your young teen now needs to learn flexibility. Teach them to maintain their goals but to be willing to divert every now and then, as the need arises. These developing young adults are usually more settled than some of their peers born under other signs but they will still want to flex their muscles occasionally. As with all other stages in this child's development, security remains important. Remember that when your child begins to challenge authority it means they are ready to take on more responsibility.

Provide them with the security and reassurance they need during this time to learn to spread their wings a little.

> Taurus is gifted with a natural voice and ear for music and they to tend to have a much higher than average success rate in the music professions, as indicated by the number of performers in the list of famous Taureans. Taurus also displays aptitudes in the professions of psychology, architecture, medicine, conservation and environment, clothing design and teaching. Your child is not so well suited to labouring jobs or IT.

The young Taurus adult

This young person is likely to have their feet fairly well planted, and as the young adult emerges they continue to work towards their goals and life plan. The young Taurean usually knows what they want to do in life and is good at setting their own goals, even if they change track later. These young adults will be keen to take total responsibility as soon as possible, although will still enjoy the home comforts and having things done for them. They will still take their time, weighing up the options before they finally begin to take action, but as with most things in life, once they have set their mind on something they will slowly but surely move towards it.

Knowing that you have faith in them and are prepared to trust them in their decision-making is very important now.

The sensual nature of Taurus means they are attracted to the more visually appealing and scented plants such as narcissus, lily-of-the-valley, rose, poppy, and apple tree.

Famous Taureans

Fred Astaire
William Shakespeare
Barbra Streisand
Shirley Temple
Orson Welles
HRH Elizabeth II
Johannes Brahms
Bing Crosby
Liberace
Carla Zampatti
Sigmund Freud
Alan Bond
Renée Zellweger
Jessica Alba
Cate Blanchett
Janet Jackson
Candice Bergen
David Beckham
Kirsten Dunst

Penélope Cruz
Daniel Johns
Jerry Seinfeld
Kelly Clarkson
Charlotte Brontë
Roy Orbison
Joe Cocker
Billy Joel
Ricky Nelson
Willie Nelson
Rita Coolidge
Ritchie Valens
Stevie Wonder
Frankie Valli
Tammy Wynette
J.M. Barrie
Pyotr Tchaikovsky
Cher
Dame Nellie Melba

Gemini child

Ruling Planet—Mercury ☿
Element—Air
Quality—Mutable
Sign—the Twins
Glyph—Ⅱ
Gemstone—Agate, all multicoloured stones
Metal—Mercury, nickel
20 May–21 June

'If evolution really works, how come mothers only have two hands?'

Milton Berle

One of the most lively and vibrant of the twelve zodiac signs, Gemini is mercurial and bright. This is the sign of Peter Pan, forever child, and anyone who knows an adult Gemini can relate to that. They are curious, talkative, social and restless. Ruled by the planet Mercury, they embody all that is represented therein. Mercury was the fleet-footed messenger of the gods. He was like quicksilver, flying here and there taking messages between the ancient gods and to the inhabitants of Earth.

Mercury was also the prankster, thus Geminis love a good joke and have a wonderful wit and sense of humour. It is also the sign of the twins and many born under this sign exhibit different sides of their personality with different people, much more than others, giving the impression they are more than one person. The Gemini child will keep you on your toes both physically and mentally. You may have difficulty keeping up with them at times but will be delighted by their antics.

Mercury is the ruling planet affecting Gemini. How it is placed in the birth horoscope will be the major influence on your child's personality and this explains why all Gemini children are not the same. The Gemini child with Mercury in Taurus will be much more grounded than the 'average' Gemini, Mercury in Gemini will add to the tendency to be a chatterbox and inquisitive, Mercury in Cancer will be more sensitive. (Mercury can never be further than one sign away from the Sun, so these are the only possible positions of this planet for the Gemini child.)

Mercury is also associated with the day Wednesday, and the number five, so your Gemini child may find them lucky.

your child's will

With a little Gemini in your home, get out your running shoes and dust the cobwebs from your brain. This little one will keep you on your toes and mentally alert. Before you know it, your little Mercurial bundle of joy will be walking and talking and running you off your feet. Their natural inquisitiveness and need for variety and change has them into everything.

The symbol for Gemini is the twins and one Gemini child can certainly feel like two. Once they start running around you may feel as though there are twins in your home. You investigate the loud crashing coming from the kitchen, only to hear something being flushed down the toilet. And you ask yourself, 'How can he be in two places at the same time?' Welcome to the world of Gemini: two for the price of one.

Observation works both ways for your child. Not only do they like to observe what is going on around them, they like to know that you are watching them as well. Be prepared for the onslaught of 'Watch me, watch me'. Your Gemini child needs the reassurance of witnesses to their achievements, to prove to themself that they can do something. Following 'Watch me, watch me', will come 'Did you see me, did you see me? I did it!'

your Gemini baby
from birth to 6 months

- Communicates using eye contact and lots of vocalisation and enjoys interaction

- Very alert and likes being talked to and to hear the sound of a human voice
- Responds well to laughter and any unusual sound
- Mirror play is good
- Loves hand and feet games—Round and round the garden, This little piggy
- Dexterous with hands and fingers
- Enjoys rhythmic movement and sound; rocking is a good way to settle baby

Needs sensory stimulation, space, mobility, interaction and conversation

Doesn't like restriction, being left alone, lack of interaction

your Gemini baby

Your Gemini baby will be bright and bubbly and very alert. This is a baby who will like to be at the centre of whatever is going on around them. Your baby is likely to sleep in short bursts and be wide awake in between. Your child will be quite content as long they can see and hear you and will enjoy being carried in a pouch for the first few months.

To help your baby into a more regular and longer sleep pattern, give them some background noise. A radio in the background can be useful, especially one that has more talk than music. Keep it on softly in your child's room so they feel they have company and are not alone. Gradually as they get older they will become more comfortable with their own thoughts and drift off to sleep much more easily.

your Gemini baby
from 6 to 18 months

- Curious and verbal, loves to talk
- Constantly in motion, short attention span, needs plenty of variety
- Begins to 'sort'; games or toys that involve sorting would be ideal at this age
- Learns through repetition and conversation
- Likely to talk and walk early
- Finds everything exciting and challenging
- Manual dexterity very good and fine motor skills tend to develop quickly
- Not likely to follow a routine

Needs space to move around and explore, independence, quiet time, variety, laughter

Doesn't like restriction, isolation, too much noise or chaos

your Gemini toddler

It is highly likely that your Gemini toddler will speak very early and be capable of holding their own in conversation with an adult by age two or three. You will find that for your child, experience needs to be verbalised before it can become real. They need to tell someone what has happened before they can store it away as a memorable experience.

Your child will be keen for independence as soon as they are capable. Once they have mastered the use of the spoon, they will protest if you continue to try and feed them. As soon as they have managed to drink from a cup they will object to being offered a bottle.

Interaction and communication are essential to your child. They will look for response and interaction, and will respond immediately to the sound of your voice. The Gemini child will begin trying to verbalise, almost from the time they are born. They will respond extremely well to the sound of laughter and any unusual or funny noise.

Your Gemini loves hand and finger games and as they get older they will delight you with their dexterity. They will also keep you amused with their verbal skills as they chatter away and try to imitate the sounds they hear. They could be a talented mimic and will be fascinated by sounds.

This child will be constantly looking to understand how something works but is more interested in the theory than the practical application. They will want to categorise and label everything they come into contact with, whether it is an inanimate object or living being. There must be some order and to achieve this there has to be a way to sort everything.

As a young child your Gemini will need variety with toys and play activities, as they have difficulty in maintaining interest for very long. When they get older you can use playtime to help extend their attention span, encouraging play for longer periods with favourite toys or activities. Geminis have a reputation for being fickle, changing their mind often or not being able to make a decision. This is in part because they are able to see both sides of an equation, and can have difficulty making a choice. This is another area where your child will need gentle guidance. Help them to make choices and let them know that it is okay to make mistakes. The earlier this training begins, the easier it becomes.

Your Gemini toddler will not enjoy being restrained and is likely to be a very restless sleeper. This can create problems trying to keep them warm during the winter months. Perhaps a roomy sleeping bag/jumpsuit would be easier than trying to keep the covers on.

Your young Gemini will enjoy cuddles and other physical contact but will not like being smothered or held too tightly.

Toilet training

Toilet training is usually a fairly fast process but can be frustrating for parents when the child seems to have grasped the concept but then relapses. Your Gemini can be so busy exploring their world that they simply forget—until it is too late. Toileting is best handled as social time to begin with. Don't leave your child on their own but make it enjoyable; talk to your child, read to them, even have a sing-song. This is also an instance where a fairly strict routine—same time, same place and where possible same people—could be of benefit. Make it fun and give as much encouragement as possible. Remember, your child is a social creature and doesn't enjoy being closed off from what is going on—that can come later.

your Gemini toddler from 18 months to 3 years

- 'Perpetual motion' could be their nickname at this age
- On the go and into everything
- Begins to perform multiple tasks at the one time

- Looks for honesty from those around them
- Will gain great satisfaction from their independence
- Mercurial personality begins to show and can become even more unpredictable

Needs feedback, conversation, quiet time, support in finishing tasks, answers and information

Doesn't like restraint, force, being ignored, repetition, may not like being tickled

your child's emotions

The Moon in a birth chart represents your child's emotions and instinctual responses. It is an excellent clue to how they respond in emotional situations. The Moon rules infancy and early childhood, and is the face of your child that you will see most often during the early years.

Emotions are also associated with the element water, as is the Moon. As the Moon waxes and wanes, we see the effects on the tides. It also affects all living beings. The Moon is instinctive, intuitive and empathetic. The Moon reflects the light from the Sun and is associated with similar attributes for your child. The Moon shows how your child deals with mood changes and emotions, how your child learns to become reflective and stores memories.

Your Gemini Moon child will be very close to any siblings they have, and if they are an only child or the only one of their gender in the family they will have a best friend who will be 'just like a sister or brother'. This child will enjoy reading and any activity that challenges their mind. They will also enjoy working with their hands.

As they don't like being cuddled too closely, a good way to settle your child when they become fractious is to talk or sing to them, as they enjoy the sound of the human voice. Your Gemini child will find the sound of your voice reassuring, and will be generally content to play on their own, as long as they can hear you.

Gemini is the first of the 'human' signs of the zodiac; the human signs do not have an animal as their symbol. This sign is also linked to Gemini's use of the mind. Arms, shoulders, hands and lungs are the most vulnerable part of the body for your Gemini child. They can be prone to allergies and asthma, especially when under stress. Usually, these are complaints they will grow out of.

Gemini is much more at home in the realms of reason, or the mind, than dealing directly with feelings. It is difficult to rationalise emotions, yet this is the way that your Gemini child deals with life. They will need your help and guidance when dealing with any emotional issues that arise. Assist them to navigate through the sea of feelings and to be at ease with their sensitivity. Not everything can be worked through at the mental level, nor is everything in life logical or black and white.

This Moon placement will generally mean that your child will not be overly fussed about their food. They can be so busy that they forget to eat at times and regular mealtimes are important. They will have a relatively simple approach to food, seeing it as a basic necessity rather than something to savour. They will tend to eat on the run unless you enforce a more regimented approach to meals. Regular healthy snacks during the day can help to supplement their tendency to rush through meals.

Gemini children enjoy the use of multiple colours, which fits their mercurial nature. Softer pastels are best, particularly when it comes to helping them settle. Bolder colours can be used for clothing or toys but should be used sparingly elsewhere.

your Gemini preschooler

Your Gemini preschooler will have a wonderful sense of humour and brilliant wit that will show itself from a young age. They will also have a wonderful imagination and ability for storytelling. They will need to learn the difference between storytelling and reality, as they can get so caught up in the telling of the story that they can exaggerate to the point where the truth somehow gets lost. They won't intentionally tell lies but there is certainly a tendency to stretch the truth a little. And like the true reporter, 'Why let the truth get in the way of a good story?' will be their attitude.

Your child's thought processes follow a logical pattern and they will usually find learning very easy, as long as the subject interests them. They can grasp reading and writing skills at quite a young age and should be a good communicator, although there can be delays in clear speech, as their mind moves too quickly for their mouth. This will eventually settle as they gradually learn to slow the pace. They will enjoy discussing a wide variety of subjects and will have a broad-ranging intellect when they are older.

Nuts and all vegetables grown above the ground (except cabbage) should excite Gemini's palate and you may find it useful to include small amounts of these in their diet. (Ensure your child is not allergic to nuts first.)

The Gemini mind is always active and for this reason your child may have difficulty sleeping, as it is difficult for them to shut down when they go to bed at night. Establish a good bedtime routine for them when they are still quite young; perhaps something like a nice, warm bath followed by a story and some quiet time to allow them to slowly wind down before you tuck them into bed. Noisy games or stories are fine during the day but not good just before bed.

They will enjoy exploring both indoors and out, as they are curious about all the world has to offer and will try to sample as much of life as possible. They will need to discipline their active mind to stay focused on one thing and move on to the next thing only after they have completed their current task.

Puzzles, number, matching and counting games and any other activity that keeps the mind occupied will be favourite pastimes for your young Gemini.

your Gemini preschooler from 3 to 6 years

- Continues to be changeable, restless and curious
- Becoming more involved with testing out different roles and truths
- Starting to develop constancy and order
- Tests parents to see if they mean what they say

- Mimicry and conversational abilities become even more highly developed
- Can be quite disconcerting with their ability to copy other members of the family
- Takes pleasure in counting, sorting and categorising things but objects to being put into a category themself
- Begins to develop skills in debating and negotiating
- Needs encouragement now with completing tasks and learning to focus on one thing until it is completed before moving to something new

Needs conversation, humour, compassion, help dealing with emotions and encouragement of imagination

Doesn't like restraint, being labelled, abandonment, too much responsibility

Fun, friendship and confidence

Your Gemini child will be more of a visual learner and will find it easier to pick up skills 'watching' how something is done, rather than 'listening' to how it is done. They have a very quick mind and assimilate knowledge and information quite easily provided they have the opportunity to 'see' how it works. They will have a tendency to want to pull things apart, so they can understand how the different parts work.

For this same reason, your child may have trouble in believing things they have not seen with their own eyes. They will enjoy looking at photographs and other visual records and it will be important for them when they get older to have a record of their childhood.

Your child will be eager to please and seek approval from others. They are also intuitive and in an effort to seek approval may only tell people what they think they want to hear.

With your Gemini child, there can be a tendency to fidget and this creates difficulty in sitting still for very long. You may also find it difficult to understand how they can do more than one thing at a time. This is a natural tendency for Gemini and as they get older don't be surprised to see them doing homework, while watching TV and at the same time listening to the radio and having a telephone conversation. Yes, they really are doing all these things at once, and in actual fact probably find it easier to concentrate while there is at least a certain amount of background distraction. One of the more difficult tasks for your child will be learning to keep their attention focused on one thing for any length of time. It would be helpful for them later in life if you can encourage them to see some activities through to completion.

Your Gemini child should find school a pleasant and exciting experience, as long as they are allowed some freedom. They will enjoy learning new skills, provided the classroom environment is not too stifling. Many Gemini children have already acquired some reading and writing skills before they start school; they are naturally curious and it is an extension of the need and desire to communicate. They are more likely to have a group of friends than one or two close friends and should be quite popular with their peers, given their charm, wit and sense of fun.

Their love of music and company makes group activities perfect for your Gemini child. Perhaps joining a choir or learning an instrument and becoming part of the local youth orchestra would be appealing for your child.

With their natural wit and way with words, Gemini can be the spokesperson for others. Bob Dylan is a Gemini who had all the answers and through his music as his chosen medium put forward his generation's message for change. Another Gemini who rose to prominence in the same era was John F. Kennedy, who was an effective agent of political change.

As your child grows, so will their curiosity and verbosity. They will require variety in their toys and play activities and enjoy puzzles and other similar activities that will stretch and expand their mind.

Gemini is associated with birds rather than mammals, and in particular parrots. These creatures of flight represent Gemini's curious and communicative nature. Geminis enjoy learning and sharing their information with others.

First impressions

The ascendant, or rising sign in your child's horoscope is where heaven meets Earth: the part of the sky that is visible on the horizon, looking directly to the east at the time of birth. Some say this represents the soul's entry into the earthly plane. In a birth chart it represents the physical body of an individual and shows how we meet the world head-on. It is referred to as the mask we wear when we first meet people, the filter through which all of the planets within the birth chart are expressed.

With Gemini on the ascendant your child will most likely have a slight build, as a young child. They may be slim-faced with large, bright sparkling eyes, and full of curiosity. When they begin to speak, they will do so, as much with their hands as with their mouth. Your child will have a bright personality; witty and clever. They may be a little highly strung and can be nervous. They will be friendly and adaptable but may be a little temperamental. Their personality can vary depending on who they are with at the time. They will have somewhat of a chameleon quality, allowing them to blend in with any crowd.

They will be happiest when they are busy, preferably with some kind of mental stimulation. The Gemini child can't bear boredom and will become quite the fidget if they don't have something to keep them occupied. They may sometimes go a little over the top with jokes and storytelling but this is usually simply a way to entertain, or a device to hide their nervousness. A valuable lesson for your Gemini child to learn is the place of silence, and that sometimes the best response is no response.

Although they are not particularly 'sporty', your child should be good at gymnastics, swimming or even marathon running: anything that combines their physical dexterity with their need for mental stimulation.

Agile of mind and body, your Gemini child will keep you on your toes mentally and physically. Their bright and bubbly nature makes them a pleasure to be around.

your Gemini child from 7 to 10 years

This is the beginning of the development of responsibility. Gemini has a tendency to move quickly from one thing to another and this can be a positive time in learning to do something well, rather than quickly.

Provide them with small tasks initially. This will give them a sense of accomplishment, and show them they can complete a task even if they become bored. Provide a suitable reward scheme, such as a daily star chart, which has a larger reward, such as a computer game, when a certain number of stars is reached. Reward charts also teach your eager Gemini child to set goals and slowly work towards them.

Your Gemini child is another who will benefit from sharing in the democracy of setting rules and the consequences for breaking them. This should preferably be negotiated together as a family and definitely before any wrongdoing occurs. Gemini is a fast learner but the application, in practical terms, usually takes much longer.

As Gemini children come under the influence of the planet Mercury, the cell salt that is most of use to them in times of stress is Kali Mur (potassium chloride). This helps to rebalance the system and can be particularly useful during puberty.

your Gemini teen from II to I4 years

As the teenager emerges, life generally becomes very hectic in the Gemini household. These developing young adults are usually very busy and there is always somewhere they need to be. As with all other stages in this child's development, the follow-through remains important.

Your Gemini teen should travel through this period relatively easily. They are not generally overly rebellious; it is more that they have a tendency to overcommit themselves. Your teen will need your guidance in only taking on what they are capable of achieving, as their tendency will be to put their hand up for whatever is going. Their willingness to try new things can leave them susceptible to experimenting with alcohol and drugs and it is important that you educate them clearly about the risks. It is also important that you encourage communication during this time, but don't harass.

It is still important to allow the emerging adult to take part in the rule-making and punishment-setting.

Gemini children have diverse interests and this is reflected in their career choices. It is common for Gemini to be a jack-of-all-trades and not unusual for them to have more than one 'career' in their lifetime. Statistically, your child has more likelihood of working with computers than with bricks or building materials. They also rank higher in the careers of journalism, higher education teachers and medicine. Your Gemini child's career choice needs to provide mental challenge and stimulation to maintain their interest. Geminis prefer to involve others rather than to work alone.

The young Gemini adult

Your emerging young adult will continue to be busy. Now on top of all their other extracurricular activities, they also have a social life! Gemini doesn't like to sit still for too long, and as the young adult emerges they will continue to sample many and varied activities. This can be a trying period, as these young adults are not all that keen to take total responsibility. It is normally not an overwhelming problem though. As always with your Gemini, keep the lines of communication open, even if it is just a grunt of acknowledgment at times, as they run to their next appointment. If you want your young Gemini adult to become responsible for themselves, it is important that you help make them responsible. That is, they need to stop long enough to take care of their basic chores, and as a parent you need to ensure they have some.

Give them support, but don't carry them. You have nurtured and encouraged their independence and responsibility up to this point, it is important that you continue now. They are still not quite ready to take the world on their own until they can at least make their own bed!

Throughout history, Gemini has been assigned to lavender, lily-of-the-valley and all nut-bearing trees. Your Gemini child may not have much of a green thumb but will enjoy the colour and scent of these plants.

Famous Geminis

Bob Dylan

John F. Kennedy

Bob Hope

Marilyn Monroe

Judy Garland

Paul McCartney

Clint Eastwood

Grant Kenny

Kylie Minogue

Pat Cash

Colleen McCullough

Angelina Jolie

Nicole Kidman
Jamie Oliver
Harriet Beecher Stowe
Mike Myers
Johnny Depp
Barry Manilow

Paula Abdul
Sir Arthur Conan Doyle
Dean Martin
William Butler Yeats
Walt Whitman

cancer child

Ruling Planet—Moon ☽
Element—Water
Quality—Cardinal
Sign—the Crab
Glyph—♋
Gemstone—Moonstone, pearl
Metal—Silver
21 June–22 July

'Each day of our lives we make deposits in the
memory banks of our children.'

Charles R. Swindoll

Cancer is a water sign and the sign under the rule of the Moon. It is associated with nurturing, both as the giver and receiver. It is reflective and intuitive. Those born under the sign of Cancer are affectionate and vulnerable and bring out the caring part of even the most hardened of adults. They are the epitome of the cute, pink, chubby and adorable baby. Gentle, sympathetic and considerate, they love to be needed.

A Cancer baby is, more than any other, in tune with the moods and rhythms of mother, or the person who takes on the major nurturing role. Your Cancer baby will be very sensitive to their environment and the moods of those around them. Mother is a very important person in their life and they may be quite clingy and unwilling to go to other people. This can include father in the very early stages and he should try not to take this personally as his time will come.

The Moon is the ruling planet affecting Cancer. How it is placed in the birth horoscope will be the major influence on your child's personality and this explains why all Cancer children are not the same. For example, the Cancer child with the Moon in Aries, Leo or Sagittarius will be much more dynamic and forceful than the 'average' Cancer, Moon in Gemini, Libra or Aquarius will tend to be more sociable, Moon in Capricorn, Taurus or Virgo will be more self-contained and grounded, while the moon in Cancer, Pisces or Scorpio will be more emotional.

The Moon is also associated with the day Monday, and the number two, so your Cancer child may find them lucky.

Your child has an ability to adjust to their surroundings and fit in well with other people. They will generally make the best of whatever situation they find themself in. This doesn't mean that they won't be inclined to the occasional whinge—they will, but having gotten it out of their system will generally move on and make the most of things.

Your child will be both shy and curious and will need encouragement to explore their environment. They will become increasingly interested in things going on around them but will still need your encouragement to participate in activities.

The Cancer child can be very determined and even though they are generally concerned for the wellbeing of others, they are not afraid of emotional blackmail if they feel it will aid their cause. Your child can also have a tendency to sulk if they feel thwarted; this is something you will need to work through. Encourage your child to talk about things and not keep them bottled up.

your cancer baby
from birth to 6 months

- Loving, sweet and hungry
- Very sensitive to environment and the moods of those around them
- Mother very important
- Shy and resistant to go to anyone other than mum
- Can have feeding problems and work best with feeding on demand and lots of cuddles

- Responds well to water and should enjoy bathtime
- May develop an affinity with the Moon, moods swing with the phases of the Moon

Needs plenty of cuddles, lots of love, plenty to eat, time with mum

Doesn't like feeling unprotected, unfamiliar places and people

your cancer baby

You have a baby that is generally quite placid and easy to manage. The Cancer baby has fairly simple needs in order to be happy: regular food and feeling secure.

Your baby will generally have a good appetite but can be prone to colic. Your baby should have quite a good sleep pattern and will enjoy being swaddled as this increases their sense of security. If they become fractious, a warm bath with a few drops of lavender oil is the easiest way to settle this little one and it is a good idea to include this in their bedtime routine.

your cancer baby from 6 to 18 months

- Timid, cute and cuddly
- Shy and curious, needs encouragement to explore their environment
- Interested in things going on around them, needs encouragement to participate
- Enjoys food but may be hesitant about trying anything new

- Water play still a favourite and bathtime can be the focus of the day
- Developing a love of nature and will enjoy walks in the park or play in the garden

Needs lots of support, encouragement and approval, protection without overprotection, lots of cuddles, private time with parents

Doesn't like being hungry or forced to eat, feeling left out

your cancer toddler

Your toddler needs plenty of cuddles, lots of love and plenty to eat. They will also need time with mum. They won't like feeling unprotected and may prefer to still be wrapped snugly to sleep. They may not enjoy any form of 'throwing' game, as in throwing them in the air, and prefer gentler play activities. Your child will also need time to adjust to unfamiliar places and people and can be on the shy side.

They will enjoy their food but may be hesitant about trying anything new. With your encouragement they will be more willing to try unfamiliar tastes and textures.

Water play and music will still be favourites as they grow and bathtime can become the focus of the day.

Your child will begin to develop a love of nature while quite small and will enjoy walks in the park or to play in the garden. They will have an affinity with animals of all kinds but particularly smaller animals when young. They could benefit from a pet from around the age of two years, preferably something small and cuddly and not too rambunctious.

As your child begins to seek their own independence they will need support, encouragement and approval. They will also need protection, without overprotection. Your child will sense your fears and if they feel there is something to be frightened of it can impede their development. Make their exploration fun and safe and you will both be happy. Your toddler won't want to appear too reliant on mum, so it can be a fine line between support and smothering.

As your little Cancer reaches toddler stage they can be emotionally erratic and this can be very disconcerting for parents. Tell yourself, 'This is just a phase, they will grow out of it eventually'.

Your child may become even less comfortable with strangers during this stage and may need your encouragement to come out of their shell, as they learn to explore the world on their own. They will be very hesitant about leaving their safety zone, and patterns established at this time can set the stage for the way they will handle new situations and demands for the rest of their life. Be gentle but firm, encourage them and praise them when they show initiative and undertake tasks on their own.

They can also become very sensitive at this stage and tend to personalise events and remarks. This means they can feel that they are the cause of anything that happens around them. They may not be very good at expressing their own needs and may instead give or do for others what they are most in need of themself. Watch for this and use it as a guide for what your child is looking for from you.

Extremely intuitive and sometimes even psychic, your little Cancer can develop an affinity with an 'imaginary' friend around this age. It is best to indulge them and definitely do not ridicule or belittle them over it. Pay heed to your Cancer child's concerns and 'feelings', which are very real to them.

Your child is also developing a tangible need for security and will create special places or things that fulfil that need: a favourite chair, toy, blanket, and so on. Their senses become very important and they will gain much experience by smelling, tasting and touching.

They will be a very sensitive child and tune in easily to the moods and emotions of those around them. Your child may be a little on the moody side and prone to brooding; however, they usually won't stay down for too long.

Toilet training

Toilet training for your Cancer child may be a long process for some, while others catch on very early and are keen to accomplish this new stage quickly. Patience and gentleness are the keys. As with most things, your Cancer child will want to please. Your child will respond best to lots of praise and attention. Ignore all mistakes or handle them discreetly, without making a big fuss. At all costs avoid embarrassing your child at this stage.

your cancer toddler
from 18 months to 3 years

- Becoming erratic and full of contradictions
- May go from rage to charm in a matter of moments
- Continues to be shy and cautious with strangers
- May become whiney

- Personalises events and remarks
- Not good at expressing own needs
- Extremely intuitive and sometimes even psychic
- May develop an affinity with an 'imaginary' friend
- Developing a need for security; will create special places or things that fulfil that need
- Senses become very important

Needs an object that symbolises security, a safe place, approval and reassurance, encouragement, calmness, lots of cuddles and other demonstrations of love, being useful

Doesn't like ridicule, to feel abandoned, criticism, feeling overwhelmed

your child's emotions

The Moon in a birth chart represents your child's emotions and instinctual responses. It is an excellent clue to how they respond in emotional situations. The Moon rules infancy and early childhood, and is the face of your child that you will see most often during the early years.

Emotions are also associated with the element water, as is the Moon. As the Moon waxes and wanes, we see the effects on the tides. It also affects all living beings. The Moon is instinctive, intuitive and empathetic. The Moon reflects the light from the Sun and is associated with similar attributes for your child. The Moon shows how your child deals with mood changes and emotions, how your child learns to become reflective and stores memories.

The Moon is at its most dignified in its own sign of Cancer. This should mean that it works well and fluidly. What can happen, though, is that the emotions can become so strong at times as to be totally overwhelming

Your child will be kind and thoughtful, constantly thinking of the needs and feelings of others. They will have an empathy with those they feel are in pain, either physically or emotionally, and can become quite distressed over the suffering of others.

One thing that is of primary importance for your child's emotional wellbeing is they won't like to throw anything away. Everything they own will have some sentimental attachment, or they believe it may come in handy one day. The worst thing you can do is to go through your child's room and throw things out. You may think you are doing them a favour but they will be devastated to lose any of their 'precious' things. This is a job that must be done together.

Like their symbol, the crab, the chest and stomach are the most vulnerable part of the body for your Cancer child. They can also be prone to tummy upsets, especially when under emotional stress.

Your child's appetite is likely to suffer if they are upset emotionally in any way and they may be prone to 'upset tummy' when they get older. If this is the case it is a good idea to identify the cause, as more often than not it is an emotional trigger—perhaps they are being bullied at school or a new baby has arrived to undermine their position. Whatever the cause, they will usually respond to an understanding hug and reassurance from parents.

They will respond well to water and music and should enjoy their bathtime, which can be a useful aid for settling them if they become overly upset. Try to make their bath the last thing before you put them down at night and you will generally find that they will settle quite easily.

Don't be surprised if they develop an affinity with the Moon and from a very early age their moods may start to swing with the phases of the Moon. Your child can be moody and is definitely sensitive, and they will also be very determined and keen to have their own way.

> Cancer children resonate to the colours sea green, silver, white, opal and iridescent hues. These are the colours of the Moon and the ocean and are indicative of their nature. If you want to promote calm around your child, utilise these colours in their room.

your cancer preschooler

Coming up to preschool age your child may become emotional and defensive. Parents sometimes have difficulty in allowing their Cancer babe to grow up and this can create dilemmas for your child. Remember, they need your encouragement and are relying on you for the signals that it is time to move on to the next stage in their development.

Their creativity is beginning to develop and imaginary friends and fantasy continue to be important to them as they develop the rich creativity that will be so much a part of their adult life.

Your child needs continued reassurance and humour along with a good dose of firm guidance and a secure emotional environment. These things will all contribute to your child's growth into a self-assured and confident adult.

Your preschooler may not have a large appetite, preferring to eat small quantities more frequently. They will enjoy their food well cooked and presented and may become quite a dab hand in the kitchen themself from a relatively young age, if you allow them to help you. Your child may have a sensitive stomach and not tolerate foods that are too spicy when younger.

Your child will prefer simple foods such as milk, fish, cabbage and fruits and vegetables with high water content. You may find it useful to include these in their diet, gradually introducing stronger-flavoured foods as they get older.

Meeting new people and going to new places are enjoyable for your child, although they can still be cautious. They will enjoy trips to the country and also the ocean. While honest and trustworthy, they may be a little 'Scrooge' when it comes to money and possessions. My little Cancer granddaughter is very aware of the monetary system and like the true Cancerian is not one to let an opportunity pass by where money is concerned. Any loose change that is lying around is immediately claimed by this alert four-year-old. She is also very protective of her 'things' and although quite generous, in that she will happily go through her toys and give them away to charity, woe betide anyone who touches any of her select 'special' toys.

Security is the most important thing in this child's life and part of that security comes from solid, tangible objects. Home is a haven to them and all of their precious little knick-knacks help to tie them to home and all those they love. They can cope with any amount of commotion outside, but within the home they need peace and harmony.

Your preschooler should sleep well and eat well, as long as they are not upset emotionally. Water and music are still ideal soothers for your child if they should become distressed. The best of all for this little one, though, is to be cuddled and held close.

your cancer preschooler from 3 to 6 years

- Emotional, defensive and at times even volatile
- Parents may have difficulty in allowing their Cancer babe to grow up
- Creativity is beginning to develop, imaginary friends and fantasy continue to to be important

Needs continued reassurance, compassion, humour, firm guidance, a secure emotional environment, to feel useful

Doesn't like ridicule, being taken too seriously, lack of security, emotional outbursts

Fun, friendship and confidence

This is one child who won't like ridicule *or* being taken too seriously. They are great mimics and love copying others. They have a wonderful sense of humour and enjoy having a good time.

Your child is uncomfortable with dishonesty, even though at times they may have their own perspective on what constitutes honesty. There is a refreshing naiveté about your child and it is probably safe to give them the benefit of the doubt, as they will usually find it difficult to lie.

They will be considerate of others, especially members of their family. For your little Cancer, part of being happy is being concerned for others. They like to take care of you and make sure everything is just right and can be quite the grown-up in this department.

Your Cancer child is a natural collector, so perhaps a hobby along these lines would be a good pastime for them, as well as utilising some of that natural urge to 'keep' things. Another area in which your child may shine is acting. Drama classes can be something that will help boost their confidence and provide another social experience. Meryl Streep, Tom Hanks, Robin Williams and Tom Cruise are just a few of the many great Hollywood Cancerians.

School is also a wonderful social experience for your child. Their attitude to school will depend on their readiness. It is important to begin preparing for this exercise long before it is time to take them for their first day. It is also important that they see you happy for them and not wanting to cling and prolong their babyhood. Encourage your child's independence and empower them to have a rewarding and enjoyable time at school.

Like their animal counterpart, the crab, Cancer tends to move sideways at the first sign of trouble. They are aware of their own vulnerability and self-protection is

usually high on their agenda. This child will generally be
non-confrontational, preferring to simply skitter out of
the way of trouble.

First Impressions

The ascendant, or rising sign in your child's horoscope is
where heaven meets Earth: the part of the sky that is visible
on the horizon, looking directly to the east at the time of
birth. Some say this represents the soul's entry into the earthly
plane. In a birth chart it represents the physical body of an
individual and shows how we meet the world head-on. It is
referred to as the mask we wear when we first meet people,
the filter through which all of the planets within the birth
chart are expressed.

Cancer on the ascendant tends to the classic 'Moon face',
as it is ruled by the Moon. Your Cancer rising child will tend
to be an attractive baby. They will generally have a well-
developed rib cage and chest and their arms are well covered.
Their skin can be a little paler than that of the rest of the
family, and height will be from average to smallish. Not being
known for their athleticism, there can be a tendency for them
to be overweight as they get older.

Kind and gentle, your child will have very close ties to
their family. They will enjoy caring for others and making
them feel comfortable, as Cancer gives a strong 'mothering'
instinct, even in males.

They will develop a strong attachment, not only to the
family, but also to the family home. They need a firm and
comfortable home base to retreat to, particularly in times of

stress. They may be the one to trace the family history, as tracing their ancestry and finding out all there is to know about their heritage will be important to them.

Like their symbol, the crab, they will retreat into the safety of their shell if they feel threatened but they also share the same tenacity and strength of purpose. Once they have their claws into an idea, they will not let go easily.

your cancer child
from 7 to 10 years

With the development of responsibility comes both freedom and fear. For your Cancer child this can be a time that encompasses both. They will be happy to have responsibility but can be fearful at standing on their own two feet.

They need to move slowly in this area but prefer not to be babied. Encourage them to become more independent and provide them with small tasks that they are totally responsible for. Your child has a natural tendency to care, so being made responsible for feeding and caring for the family pet can be a positive task for them to take on. Support them initially according to what they need, but don't do their job for them.

Your child has a strong desire to please and make you happy, so they should work through this phase quite well with your support. Reassure them that you are still there should they need you but they are now becoming more capable of taking care of the little things themself. Simple tasks such as making their own bed, picking up after themself and even helping to cook the family meal are all useful ways for them to learn more about personal responsibility.

As Cancer children come under the influence of the Moon, the cell salt that is most of use to them in times of stress is Calc Fluor (calcium fluoride). This is useful in rebalancing the system, particularly under emotional tension, and can be especially useful during puberty.

your cancer teen from II to I4 years

As the teenager emerges, life can become emotional in the Cancer household. Your child doesn't become any less caring but can be awash with conflicting emotions as puberty hits and takes hold. The cheerful outgoing Cancer child can become a very sullen and withdrawn teenager. They want their freedom and independence but are at the same time fearful of losing the comfort of parental support. As with earlier stages, what they need most is your continued support and understanding, coupled with gentle encouragement to make their own decisions in life.

It is important not to belittle them or do anything that can undermine their developing sense of self at this point, as they will very quickly withdraw into their shell. A Cancer adolescent who seeks the shelter of their own shell can be very difficult to prise out again.

When it comes to vocational choices, your Cancer child could do well in almost any profession, as statistically they seem to be fairly evenly spread. They will be naturally drawn to any 'caring' type profession and tend to be more highly represented in fields such as social work and teaching. They come in way below average for any of the 'labouring' professions such as builders, bricklayers, etc. Cancer is also well represented in the acting field, with the likes of Tom Hanks, Geoffrey Rush and Kathy Bates among the more successful Cancerian thespians. This is a reflection of their amazing ability to mimic others and take on different personas.

The young cancer adult

As the young adult emerges, so does the Cancer emerge from their shell. You will notice the change as your rather shy child becomes a more confident and social individual. The young Cancer can still be on the shy side but is now more willing to be drawn out and participate on a wider playing field.

What is important as a parent through this stage, is that you are watchful that your child doesn't swing too far the other way and abandon their sense of responsibility. This is something that will need to be monitored. Your young adult can be so keen to join the 'social set' that they forget who they are and can lose themself for a while.

Encourage them in their new-found confidence but remind them occasionally of their responsibilities, especially if they are still studying. Your child remains the sensitive soul they have always been but can become 'crabby' while coming to terms with the adult world.

Throughout history, Cancer has been assigned to the white rose, lily, geranium, and all white flowers and these can help to bring a sense of peace into your child's environment.

Famous Cancerians

Harrison Ford

Gough Whitlam

Barbara Cartland

Meryl Streep

Nelson Rockefeller

John Farnham

Judith Durham

Mal Meninga

Bryan Brown

Princess Diana

Prince William

Lindsay Lohan

Liv Tyler

Jessica Simpson

Jo Frost

Chris Isaak

Tobey Maguire

Geoffrey Rush

Tom Hanks

Robin Williams

Kathy Bates

Missy Elliott

Jack Dempsey

Mike Tyson

Tom Cruise

George Orwell

Leo child

Ruling Planet—Sun ☉
Element—Fire
Quality—Fixed
Sign—the Lion
Glyph—♌
Gemstone—Ruby
Metal—Gold
22 July–22 August

'Hope is a world of rich vibrant colours, lively music and endless possibilities, without these there is naught but misery and bleakness.'

the author

Leo is the sign of the Sun and those born under this sign are warm and loving, and, just as their ruling planet, like to shine. The Leo child is bright and sunny and loves attention and affection. They are resilient, courageous and friendly and will seek attention in any form. If positive attention is not forthcoming, your Leo child will turn to negative behaviour to gain the needed attention.

Your child will be bright, entertaining, delightful and generous. Generosity is one of the key words for Leo, as it is in their nature to share, both in a material sense and a spiritual one. They will share their possessions and quite often give things away if they feel that someone else would be made happy by their actions. Your child asks for nothing more than to be loved and recognised. Their warmth will radiate to all who come into contact with them.

The Sun itself is the ruling planet for Leo. How it is supported by other planets in the birth horoscope will be the major influence on your child's personality. For example, the Leo child with strong Saturn will be more reserved and responsible, whereas a strong aspect to Uranus makes for a more independent and sometimes unpredictable personality.

The Sun is also associated with the day Sunday, and the number one, so your Leo child may find them lucky.

your child's will

Your child's desire for attention and affection can lead them to be susceptible to flattery and they may become cynical from a young age if they are manipulated in this way. Your child needs consistent and genuine praise for their accomplishments, to be recognised when they have worked hard for something and not to be taken for granted.

Your Leo child can be quite stubborn when they have set their mind on a particular path and force will just make them dig their heels in further. They can be talked around with rational arguments and this is always the best way to go with your Leo child. Bullying will not work.

Your child will have a natural tendency to be warm and outgoing but has a fragile ego. Once they feel crushed, your child will be unwilling to test the waters again. While you need to give your child guidance, it is best to do so in a way that does not belittle them or undermine their self-confidence.

your Leo baby from birth to 6 months

- Sunny and loving
- Generally very healthy
- Enjoys being the centre of attention
- Vocal and demanding—becoming even more so if needs are not met immediately
- Physically and emotionally strong
- Loves fun and 'magic' games, bouncing, peek-a-boo, tickling and 'copy cat' type play
- Is stimulated by sight more than sound

Needs plenty of praise, love, physical contact and attention

Doesn't like being ignored

your Leo baby

The Leo baby is one of the 'easier' babes to care for, despite their tendency to be demanding. As with fellow fire signs, Aries and Sagittarius, your Leo baby will be warm and friendly, greeting you with a welcoming smile. They will enjoy being in your company and seek to engage you in eye contact. Your baby responds better to visual than auditory cues. They will enjoy being surrounded by richly coloured toys and playthings and enjoy bright, sparkly things. A mirror is also a good plaything, but make sure it is not breakable. They will enjoy babbling away to their own reflection and this also allows them the opportunity of testing out new facial expressions.

Your baby will be generally a reasonably good sleeper and feeder, with nothing exceptional one way or the other in this department. They will be quite alert when awake and can be quite an active baby, moving around a lot. By the time they reach six months they will want to be included in everything that is going on around them. They will tend to be impatient at becoming independent, in rolling, sitting, crawling and wanting to feed themselves as soon as possible. They will respond very early to any show of love and affection and return it with a warm smile and gurgles of contentment.

your Leo baby
from 6 to 18 months

- Alert and curious
- Loves discovery and likes to share with others
- Enjoys showing off for people
- Needs plenty of interaction from others

- Looks for approval
- Becoming aware of 'personal' power and the effect they can have on their immediate environment
- Aware of the responses they get from others, will experiment with cause and effect on a personal level

Needs attention, approval, appropriate responses, socialising and sharing

Doesn't like being ignored, disapproval or limits

your Leo toddler

Initially you will see your child's sunny and loving personality. Leo children are generally healthy and robust; their sense of optimism also makes them fairly resilient. They may fall prey to the usual childhood ills but recover very quickly. Unless there are indications to the contrary, your Leo child will have a relatively strong constitution.

Your child will be amusing and charming and will delight you with their antics and attention-seeking manoeuvres. The thing to remember, above all, is that your child needs to be loved and to know it. Their attention-seeking is a way of allowing you to show how much you love them. This is something that will appear from a very young age and will continue into old age. To this end they enjoy being the centre of attention but prefer it in a positive way and on their own terms.

While they may drive you crazy at times, you can guarantee the moment you ask them to 'put on a show' they will clam up. If you want grandma to see their latest achievement, allow them to do it themself. The worst mistake you can make is to say something like, 'She's crawling now. Show grandma how clever you are.' You will end up with egg on your face as they sit in one spot looking at you as though you are crazy. They love to put themself on show but hate being 'put on show'.

Popular perception typecasts Leos as the dominant 'stars' of Hollywood and the entertainment industry, but statistically this just isn't the case. While Leo stars are very noticeable, there aren't that many. Their need for attention comes from a different space. They prefer a more intimate audience and perform for their own pleasure and for those they are close to.

As well as being physically strong, they are also emotionally strong, at least on the surface. They are very sensitive and easily hurt but will cover it up with bravado, or worse, by some form of negative response. They will develop a very strong sense of self, if they are encouraged to express themself and allowed the freedom to try out different scenarios. On the other hand, if they are put down or made to feel that it isn't appropriate to show themself, they will become withdrawn and find it difficult as an adult to allow their sunny side to be seen.

Your child will love fun and 'magic' games such as bouncing, peek-a-boo, tickling and 'copy cat' type play. They are as enchanted by their surroundings as they are enchanting and make-believe and role-playing will keep them amused for hours on end. They enjoy laughter and will develop a good sense of humour. Your child will develop a wonderful ability to laugh at themself but can become very embarrassed if others laugh at them first.

They love discovery and like to share their finds with others. They are very much a communal child and while they like to be noticed they need to be like everyone else, and to feel accepted, even at this tender age.

Your Leo child looks for approval, particularly from those closest to them, and because of this there is really no need for any form of harsh discipline. If they feel they have done something that you don't approve of, they will do their best not to repeat the mistake. They need your approval and will strive as much as possible to obtain this.

By the age of two, they are becoming aware of their 'personal' power and the effect they can have on their immediate environment. They are aware of the responses they get from others and are experimenting with cause and effect on a personal level. The best way to handle this stage is to reward their positive behaviour while ignoring (where suitable) their more negative behaviour, remembering that one of the things they fear most is to be ignored.

As a toddler they will also want to share their love and happiness with those around them and continue to be very affectionate and seek out physical contact. They will shower those in their immediate circle with all manner of little gifts that they have collected or made. When you receive one of these gifts, make sure you show them the appreciation they deserve, remembering that no matter the offering, it comes truly from their little heart of gold.

Toilet training

Toilet training is handled best by mum or another female. Leo is fastidious and likes privacy. At the same time they will respond well to praise and will react favourably to having a huge fuss made over them. If the response is consistent they will train themself very quickly to experience the approval of those they love.

your Leo toddler
from 18 months to 3 years

- Bright, entertaining, delightful and generous
- Loving and tender, may mimic adults
- Can be quite dramatic and tend to exaggeration
- Girls at this stage would quite often prefer to be boys
- Normally cheerful, may become cranky and controlling when not given their own way
- Rebellious and contrary as they begin testing limits
- Can be bossy with other children
- Can usually be brought out of a bad mood with humour

Needs plenty of attention, approval, support and encouragement, reasonable limits, reassurance that someone is in control

Doesn't like being ignored or forgotten, losing control, public humiliation

your child's emotions

The Moon in a birth chart represents your child's emotions and instinctual responses. It is an excellent clue to their response in emotional situations. The Moon rules infancy and early childhood, and is the face of your child that you will see most often during the early years.

Emotions are also associated with the element water, as is the Moon. As the Moon waxes and wanes, we see the effects on the tides. It also affects all living beings. The Moon is instinctive, intuitive and empathetic. The Moon reflects the light from the Sun and is associated with similar attributes for your child. The Moon shows how your child deals with mood changes and emotions, how your child learns to become reflective and stores memories.

Your Leo child's emotional security will come simply from knowing that they are loved. They will want to be the centre of your attention and to have your adoration. As they will be such a warm and loving child, this shouldn't be too hard. They will be very confident within the home environment and where they feel comfortable but may be a little hesitant outside of their safety zone.

Like their animal counterpart, the lion, Leo is courageous and daring. In accordance with this, the heart and spine are the most vulnerable parts of the body for your Leo child. Teach them to walk through life with their head high and their spine straight, for both spiritual and physical wellbeing.

They will have a tendency to be somewhat dramatic in their speech and actions and nothing that happens in their life will be minor, in their eyes. When your child falls and grazes their knee, you will have to bring out the full medical kit as nothing less will satisfy them. It will be a different story, however, if something major or serious does happen, as their pride will kick in then and you will see a whole different side to them.

They will try very hard at anything they do, as they will constantly be seeking your approval. When they bring home their latest painting from preschool for you to admire, just watch how crestfallen they become if you ignore it or, worse still, criticise. In their eyes they have created this wonderful work of art for you and if they feel you don't approve of their work, they also feel you don't approve of them.

Leo children resonate to the colours orange, gold, rich yellows and royal purple and these can be particularly useful to lift their mood. When they are overstimulated or difficult to settle, a touch of calming green, pink or blue can help soothe them.

your Leo preschooler

The Leo child will be fairly resilient and have the ability to recover from setbacks or disappointments fairly quickly. Their sunny nature means they will not be held down for too long. Their natural exuberance and determination will mean that they will very rarely be sidetracked once they have set their mind to something. This same determination can lead to stubbornness on occasion.

Your child will be intensely loyal and proud of those they love, including their friends, but has a tendency to 'hero worship' and becomes bitterly disappointed when they discover the object of their worship is only human after all.

They need space and won't enjoy being cramped in for too long. If they share a room, try to create their own space where they can keep all of their 'precious' objects. Your Leo preschooler can be quite vocal and demanding and become even more so if they feel their needs are not being met quickly enough. Never forget they are royalty and you will get along very well.

Your child will mimic adults around them with their dolls, animals or other children as they learn to care for themself and others. Role-playing is an integral component of their development and while for the most part they will stick to copying the same-sex parent, there will also be times when they try the role of the opposite sex. This is perfectly normal and important for them to be able to develop a full understanding of all of the facets of their own nature.

You can also expect your child to be quite dramatic and tend to exaggeration at times. They may need guidance in knowing when to embellish for the sake of a good story and when to keep to the facts. The worst injury your child is likely to sustain is to their pride, which is probably their most fragile aspect.

Although they are normally cheerful they may become cranky and controlling when not given their own way. They like to be in control and when they feel they are losing this, the real drama will begin to show itself. They also can become rebellious and contrary as they begin testing limits; they need to know just how far they can push. They can usually be brought out of a bad mood with humour and love to laugh.

They can be bossy with other children and need to learn that everyone needs to have a turn at being the boss and that they can't always have things their own way. They like to be popular, so point out to them that they will be liked more if they sometimes do things others want to do; they will readily comply.

your Leo preschooler
from 3 to 6 years

- Enjoys playing at 'grown-ups'
- Enjoys drama and is now able to use exaggeration for entertainment of others
- Will mirror the behaviour of adults around them
- Needs encouragement and approval to show a less cheery face when necessary
- Loving and generous
- Social and outgoing
- While friendly, may appear arrogant or snobbish
- May tease or boss other children while testing out leadership skills
- Likes to win
- Girls will try to prove they are as good, fast, clever, strong, etc. as boys

Needs to be included, praise, approval, support, compassion and honesty

Doesn't like being left out, being humiliated (especially in public), feeling unimportant, having to act too grown up or too much responsibility, being wrong

Fun, friendship and confidence

Making friends will be no problem for your child as they get older, as their natural warmth and exuberance will make them popular with their peers. They may run into difficulties if they don't learn to control their desire to rule the roost, though. They can forgive most faults in others but are very unforgiving if they feel that they have been personally slighted.

They will enjoy most activities, both indoors and outdoors. They will be naturally sporty, and although not aggressively competitive their pride will push them to achieve. They are also artistic and creative, and music, art, dance and theatre could also have a strong appeal.

Their feelings are intense and therefore they tend to create drama around them. They will do anything for those they love but need their efforts to be appreciated. They are very sociable and enjoy the company of other people. They will seek to be the centre of attention within their own home or familiar surroundings. Their warmth and generosity of spirit make them very easy to love and they are willing to share it with everyone they come into contact with. When this little one hugs you, you know you have been hugged.

As your child tests out their leadership skills, they may tease or boss other children and once again need guidance in appropriate behaviour when this happens. Leos are natural leaders but they need to develop their skills when young in order to prevent them growing into dictators.

They will also be very competitive and need to learn to be a good loser, as they cannot win all the time. Once again, it will be their pride that is most damaged and they will just need some time to themself to regain their composure. Your Leo girl will also try to prove she is as good, fast, clever and strong as boys—or anyone else, for that matter.

The lion is the animal associated with Leo and the 'King of the Beasts' represents your child's pride and desire to be noticed. It also represents the courage and certainty with which your child faces the world.

First impressions

The ascendant, or rising sign in your child's horoscope is where heaven meets Earth: the part of the sky that is visible on the horizon, looking directly to the east at the time of birth. Some say this represents the soul's entry into the earthly plane. In a birth chart it represents the physical body of an individual and shows how we meet the world head-on. It is referred to as the mask we wear when we first meet people, the filter through which all of the planets within the birth chart are expressed.

With Leo on the ascendant, your child will be tall and well built (within the family norm), with an abundant head of hair. They will have a regal way about them when they walk. They will have something of a leonine look about them; a broad forehead and nose are quite common with Leo, as well as prominent cheekbones.

Your child will hold their head high when they walk, with a slow measured pace, like a lion prowling. They may appear aloof and even arrogant to outsiders, but this is just their natural appearance and not intentional. They will have a warm and sunny personality but can be a little shy and stand-off-ish at times.

Your child will enjoy being the centre of attention, but particularly of your attention. They may not always seek the limelight but will usually handle it well when it happens. Their warm personality ensures that they will never be short of friends. Your child will enjoy working at a steady, rather than hurried pace and will like to do things in their own time. They don't like being rushed and can become quite irritable and even angry if this happens.

> Your Leo child's natural warmth and friendliness means they will enjoy having a pet and should have a natural affinity to cats, although Leo generally isn't too choosy and seems to like most animals.

your Leo child from 7 to 10 years

From age seven onwards your child's sense of right and wrong develops quite rapidly. It is important to trust your child and help them develop their sense of fairness. They may not be so good at carrying out a task but this age encompasses the development of responsibility. Provide them with small tasks that are their responsibility and reward them with suitable praise for accomplishment. Remember not to ridicule or belittle your child if they don't accomplish a set task. Your child will seek your approval above all else and will do their best to please, so begin with things you know they are capable of achieving.

Introduce your child to the democracy of setting rules and the consequences for breaking those rules. Your Leo child is more likely to take an autocratic approach to discipline, meaning they will be quick to point out when others have broken the rules and what punishment should apply but not so keen on the same treatment for themself. If they take part in the rule-setting and suitable punishment they are less likely to complain, although they may still sulk.

> As Leo children come under the influence of the Sun, the cell salt that is most of use to them in times of stress is Mag Phos (magnesium phosphate). This is useful to ease nervous tension and can be particularly useful during puberty.

your Leo teen from 11 to 14 years

As the teenager emerges, so does the drama increase in the Leo household. Your teen will not necessarily be a rebel, but they can increase the demand for attention. Everything in your child's life can become akin to a scene from a soap opera during this stage of their development. It is important that you don't allow yourself to become a part of the drama that is continually playing itself out, as your child will need someone to remain calm and give them the firm grounding they are looking for.

Your teenager needs firm boundaries and rules at this point and allowing them to take part in rule-setting is still worthwhile, although you will need to take a stronger role. Your young lion or lioness may have a rather skewed idea of what constitutes justice and is likely to try to always swing the balance in their favour. As the parent you will need to remain firm but fair.

Career choices for your Leo child will tend to be more along the executive or management line. Statistically, they are likely to be among those who own their own company, showing the Leo desire to be the boss. Leo also figures highly among painters and in law and pharmaceuticals. They have a significantly lower showing among bricklayers, farmers and white- and blue-collar professions. Whichever field your child chooses, they will need a certain amount of responsibility and opportunity to show their entrepreneurial skills.

The young Leo adult

The emerging Leo adult may not be so quick to take responsibility for themself. Parties and the social scene will have a large role to play and the main bone of contention between parent and child will be over the amount of time spent on their social life, versus the time they should be spending on study. These young adults will be slow to take total responsibility, preferring the home comforts and having things done for them.

It continues to be important as the parent that you maintain firm guidelines and boundaries. Your young adult needs to be encouraged to take on independence and responsibility. Teach them how to have the good things they want from life by working towards them on their own. Your child has the ability to inspire others and this will ensure they are able to create a viable network around them but they need to be prepared to do the grunge work as well.

Your Leo child will love all yellow flowers, such as sunflower, marigold and calendula. Perhaps you can plant some together in the garden or in a pot for them to enjoy.

Famous Leos

Princess Margaret
Lucille Ball
Eddie Fisher
Alfred Hitchcock
Jacqueline Kennedy
Walter Brennan
Carl Jung
Robert Burns
Cecille B. DeMille
Sir Walter Scott
George Bernard Shaw
Mae West

Sandra Bullock
Jennifer Lopez
Ben Affleck
Robert Redford
Madonna
Missy Higgins
J.K. Rowling
Daniel Radcliffe
Emily Brontë
Alfred Tennyson
Louis Armstrong
Herman Melville

virgo child

Ruling Planet—Mercury ☿
Element—Earth
Quality—Mutable
Sign—the Virgin
Glyph—♍
Gemstone—Sardonyx
Metal—Mercury, nickel
22 August–22 September

'To accomplish great things, we must not only act,
but also dream; not only plan, but also believe.'

Anatole France

Those born under the sign of Virgo are inquisitive, dexterous, particular, and seek perfection. Virgo is an earth sign, mutable in quality and ruled by the planet Mercury. In the search for perfection Virgos can be critical, both of themselves and others. They are noted for being 'picky' and have a reputation for being super-fussy. They are generally health-conscious and this can develop into obsession if taken too far. Virgo is probably the most body-conscious of all signs and the Virgo child needs time and privacy to become acquainted with their own body, developing realistic expectations of their body and their own physical limitations. They will seek perfection in themself and try to be the perfect child. They may feel inadequate and even a failure if they are unable to live up to the expectations they set for themself.

Mercury is the ruling planet affecting Virgo. How it is placed in the birth horoscope will be the major influence on your child's personality and this explains why all Virgo children are not the same. The Virgo child with Mercury in Leo will be much more outgoing and chatty than the 'average' Virgo, Mercury in Libra will tend to be more socially inclined, while Mercury in Virgo will emphasise the more pedantic and analytic nature. (Mercury can never be further than one sign away from the Sun, so these are the only possible positions of this planet for the Virgo child.)

Mercury is also associated with the day Wednesday, and the number five, so your Virgo child may find them lucky.

your child's will

Your little Virgo will be hard-working, conscientious and well organised. They will generally be modest and a little on the shy side and will try their hardest at everything they do. They will be practical and down to earth, dependable and realistic. They are very competent, analytical and aim for workmanship of the highest quality. They like to pay attention to detail, a trait they can sometimes carry too far, becoming fussy and critical. They can have difficulty working on large projects as they become so bogged down with the fine details they lose track of the final goal. It is therefore better to give Virgo tasks that are divided into small components.

If you want an honest opinion, ask your little Virgo but don't complain when they give it to you. They will tend to be frank and speak their mind honestly. They will enjoy the company of a small pet such as a kitten or bird; this will allow them to express their love while at the same time catering to their need to care for a dependant. They would not cope very well with a large, energetic dog.

your virgo baby from birth to 6 months

- Sweet and serious
- Undemanding and adaptable
- Enjoys being held and cuddled
- Cries when in physical distress and requires changing immediately they become wet or soiled
- Responds better to routine than the unexpected
- Observant and alert

Needs cuddles, being clean, routine, eye contact, interaction, soft clothing

Doesn't like physical discomfort, surprises

your virgo baby

Your Virgo baby needs routine and regularity more than any other. This baby will do well with routine feeding times and will be most settled if bath and bed times are also regular. They will become distressed very quickly if left wet or soiled and need their basic maintenance taken care of immediately. They can be fussy feeders and may have sensitive skin, so take care with your baby wash and washing powder.

When introducing solids with your baby, do so one taste at a time. Your baby will take to their food better if it contains no lumps at all initially and the taste is relatively bland. When your baby is comfortable with their solids you can gradually add variety and texture but it is still best to offer the foods one flavour at a time. So don't mix the peas with the pumpkin or carrots with potato, but serve each food individually; even if it doesn't seem right to your taste, it will be for your baby.

your virgo baby
from 6 to 18 months

- Becoming methodical
- Enjoys pulling things apart and putting them back together; will enjoy toys such as stacking cups, blocks and large Lego bricks
- Alert and curious, taking note of everything that is happening around them

- Likely to begin talking early and become intrigued with labels
- Enjoys nature and will begin to show a deep feeling and respect for both animals and plants
- Will enjoy being outdoors but may react to changes in temperature
- Will explore cautiously and is generally quite careful, fearing injury

Needs stimulating toys, communication, cuddles, encouragement, choices

Doesn't like hurting themself, making mistakes, the unexpected

your virgo toddler

Your toddler will be very sensitive to any form of criticism, and you need to give them correction gently. They will be very easy to discipline, as they want nothing more than to please you. They are highly unlikely to be too boisterous or rowdy or do anything to deliberately cause you upset. They will try their hardest to be a 'perfect' child. It is important that you start as early as possible to let them know that you don't want, or expect perfection from them. They will demand this from themself anyway and are prone to put too much pressure on themself to perform well in everything they do.

They will be a very serious and focused child, may begin to talk at an earlier age than their peers, and will converse at a level beyond their years. Their vocabulary may well amaze you and they will enjoy discussing all manner of subjects. They will be fascinated by all the finer details of a subject and are likely to ask 'how' more often than 'why'.

Your child will prefer simple and nutritious foods. As soon as they are old enough they will let you know what they do and don't like and exactly how they want their food prepared. They are quite fussy in this area but not difficult. If you are able to tune into their preferences, they are very easy to please most of the time.

They will enjoy music and will love to read as they get older. You can begin reading to them from as young as a few months old (earlier if you prefer). This will introduce them to a recreation that they will enjoy all of their life, and at this early age they will enjoy listening to the melody in your voice as you read. This can be a wonderful bonding time as they cuddle in to listen. As they are not likely to be a super-cuddly child as they get older, this can be an important time for establishing physical contact.

Your child will be honest and pay careful attention to details, although they can become so caught up in the fine details that they are unable to see the big picture. They will be efficient and dependable and enjoy helping around the house. They are both serious and friendly, but remember that they are also likely to be very shy and are definitely sensitive. They will take all criticism to heart so there is a need to be very careful when correcting this little one.

Your little one will amaze you at times with the wisdom they utter; these children are generally wise beyond their years. You will also find that right from the beginning your child will have very definite ideas on what they do and do not like. Even if you are left scratching your head over the fact that they eat all of their spinach or brussels sprouts but won't touch the bowl of ice-cream you offer them for dessert. There will be no cajoling or convincing your Virgo child to eat something they don't want. Mealtimes will be where you notice most how fussy your child can be, although their fussiness will not be confined to just their eating habits.

Your child will like to be kept clean and tidy. This is one little child who will not be comfortable playing in the dirt unless they are able to wash their hands and change their clothes immediately if they become soiled. They will also prefer to have their room kept neat and tidy, and all their toys neatly in place.

Toilet training

This will go quite smoothly if you use clear and reasonable explanations and reason. They will be eager to accomplish this skill to stay clean and comfortable and unless there is some physiological problem, your Virgo child usually gets through this process easily and quickly. Occasional accidents may occur as they become so engrossed in other activities they forget. In this case, respond with as little fuss as possible and if they are expected to clean up after themself, quietly, they will very quickly learn to pay more attention to their physical needs. Discretion and privacy, along with clear explanations of what is required, will see your little Virgo accomplish this skill in an easy and quick fashion.

your virgo toddler from 18 months to 3 years

- Shy and curious, quietly seeking out information
- Intelligent and intense, constantly asking questions and integrating information

- Remaining cautious, they value organisation and may develop their own rituals
- May be hesitant at trying out new skills until they feel they can do the task well
- If they didn't speak early they will now begin speaking in full sentences
- Enjoys being helpful, particularly with little tasks around the home
- Likely to become curious about health, illness and their own body

Needs honest reasons and explanations, cuddles, experimentation, room for error, encouragement to play and have fun, limits, choices

Doesn't like chaos (unless it is of their own making), lack of information, being pushed beyond their abilities, lack of boundaries, dirt

your child's emotions

The Moon in a birth chart represents your child's emotions and instinctual responses. It is an excellent clue to how they respond in emotional situations. The Moon rules infancy and early childhood, and is the face of your child that you will see most often during the early years.

Emotions are also associated with the element water, as is the Moon. As the Moon waxes and wanes, we see the effects on the tides. It also affects all living beings. The Moon is instinctive, intuitive and empathetic. The Moon reflects the light from the Sun and is associated with similar attributes for your child. The Moon shows how your child deals with mood changes and emotions, how your child learns to become reflective and stores memories.

The Virgo Moon will tend to quieten down your child's personality somewhat. Your child will favour the practical side, rather than the emotional. They will try to rationalise a situation and will ask questions in an emotional situation rather than simply reacting to it. It is important that you remember your child is nevertheless experiencing emotions and needs support and time to work things through.

Your child will gain emotional security and satisfaction in tangible, practical ways. They may not express their love verbally or even physically but will try to do little things to help you as a way of showing you how they feel. They will look for similar things from you as a sign that you love them also.

Your Virgo child is most vulnerable in the stomach and bowels and can suffer from nervous complaints in these areas. They are also susceptible to allergies.

They will still enjoy cuddles and other signs of affection from you but will look for the things you do for them. Little things like keeping them clean and fresh, having their room neat and tidy, preparing their food the way they like are all things that will reinforce them emotionally. They will prefer to be clean and you should never leave a soiled bib on your little Virgo. Once they have finished their meal, take off any clothing that has spilled food on it and wipe their face and hands well.

Your child can be quite shy and will tend to be hesitant and reserved when it comes to making friends and meeting new people. Despite this, they will enjoy company as they get older, particularly those who are intelligent and witty conversationalists. They are actually quite sociable but lacking a little in confidence.

Virgo children resonate to earthy colours; dark browns, greens and navy blue are their best colours. They could do with an occasional boost of more vibrant colours such as reds and orange when their energy levels are low, and a touch of paler calming green or blue can help soothe them.

your Virgo preschooler

Lots of love and physical touch for the little Virgo child helps them to become comfortable with their own body. This is a very important part of your child's growing up as they are the most health-conscious and body-conscious of all the Sun signs. They have a very strong sense of physical boundaries and could become quite upset with unnecessary probing and poking, such as fingers probing their mouth for new teeth.

Being overly concerned with this little one's health and growth could lead them to believe as they grow older that they are fragile or have a physical ailment. As health issues will be of prime importance to them, it is essential that they learn a sensible health regime as they grow, otherwise they may become fanatical. Health-wise, your little one is fairly robust physically although there could be a tendency towards allergies, plus occasional stomach upsets and colic. They may be prone to nervous headaches or stomach aches, as they will have a tendency to be a bit of a worrier.

The foods most useful for your child are potatoes, carrots, turnips and all root vegetables, also nuts of all varieties. You may find it useful to include small amounts of these in their diet once their palate is mature enough to appreciate them. (Ensure first they do not have an allergy to nuts.)

Your preschooler will be very particular about their possessions. They also like to follow a routine and can become quite upset if the right thing doesn't happen at the right time. This is definitely one child who benefits from a scheduled routine: they like to know that everything and everyone is in their rightful place at the correct time. Try to keep things such as bathtime, mealtimes and bedtime as regular as possible. If you want to encourage your child to be more adventurous and adaptable, it is better to try other times and other activities. You could do things like change their playtime or play activities if you wish to encourage them in this area. They will enjoy going for walks and this is a good habit to encourage as they grow, as it is also good for their health. Perhaps you could vary the time of day when you take your walk or where you go.

Your Virgo child will also enjoy working with their hands, drawing, painting, building, and working in the garden or in the kitchen. These activities are not only pleasurable for them, they are also the ideal opportunity for you to give them a lot of praise and encouragement; all vital for their self-esteem. They will enjoy working with adults and as they are unlikely to ask for attention, these kinds of activities are an ideal way to share time with them and show your love. Try to remember that no matter how self-sufficient they appear to be or how grown-up they try to be, your Virgo child needs constant reassurance and expressions of love.

They will have high expectations of themself and others and can set themself up for disappointment. Your child will tend to be modest and unassuming, preferring to work behind the scenes rather than in the limelight. They will have a serious attitude when it comes to learning and will be able to retain an incredible amount of information on a wide range of subjects. They will make an ideal partner in a game of Trivial Pursuit when they are a little older.

your virgo preschooler
from 3 to 6 years

- Usually modest and cautious
- Enjoys working out problems and fixing things
- Likes trying out new ideas or solutions and enjoys sharing these with others
- Would prefer to share ideas than feelings
- Can become irritable or fidgety if scared or nervous and needs to be taught how to express their feelings and that it is okay to feel this way
- Needs encouragement to be themself
- Will always be kind and gentle but occasionally may need to be reminded of these qualities within themself if they get stuck in one of their more negative moods

Needs experimentation, doing things their own way, honest responses, guidance, choices and alternatives

Doesn't like criticism, disappointment

Fun, friendship and confidence

Your child would prefer to be busy, preferably with useful tasks and will glow when you praise them for being so clever. When looking for toys and games for your child, look for those that have some purpose. These include puzzles, building sets, a miniature kitchen or workbench. When your child gets older, microscope and chemistry sets will keep them occupied for hours. They will prefer a light and sunny place to play and won't like a dark room or loud and noisy games or people.

They have a quick and sharp mind and learning to read and write and do basic maths should be no problem to them. Giving them lots of praise for their efforts and not just their 'successes' will help them to be a little less demanding of themself. Let them know how much you love them, often, as your Virgo child needs constant reassurance.

With a quick, active and inquiring mind your Virgo child will enjoy reading books and doing focused tasks on their own. They will need your encouragement to develop confidence to play with other children, otherwise they may spend too much time alone and not enough learning social skills. Your child will tend to prefer to play one-on-one with other children rather than in a large group, and organising play dates for them will help with their social skills and their confidence.

Their health will be generally good, although they may be prone to allergy-related problems such as asthma, eczema or hay fever. Their nerves are likely to be more of a problem than any physical ailment and they may be prone to hypochondria.

You have a sensitive child who will set themself high goals. It is important to boost their self-esteem and teach them that nobody is perfect, that they should always try their best but be content with their own achievement and not rely on the judgment of others.

Virgo has an association with the monkey, among other animals, and this represents the busyness of Virgo as well as their dexterity.

First impressions

The ascendant, or rising sign in your child's horoscope is where heaven meets Earth: the part of the sky that is visible on the horizon, looking directly to the east at the time of birth. Some say this represents the soul's entry into the earthly plane. In a birth chart it represents the physical body of an individual and shows how we meet the world head-on. It is referred to as the mask we wear when we first meet people. The filter through which all of the planets within the birth chart are expressed.

With Virgo on the ascendant, your child will be attractive. Their skin is usually quite beautiful, although they may be prone to acne during their teenage years. Your child may be a little taller than average, tending to the slender side, with good posture.

They will tend to be practical and objective, with a good eye for fine detail. Your child will be on the quiet side, a little shy and somewhat unassuming. They will be polite and guarded when meeting someone for the first time but will be generous and kind and enjoy helping other people. This is a child who will gain great enjoyment from helping you with little chores around the house.

There may be a tendency, as they get a little older, to be a little hard on themself. Your child tends to be a natural worrywart and will fuss endlessly to make sure that they look just right. They could also be a little on the nervy side and be a real fidget, finding it difficult to sit still for very long.

Your child will tend to be a perfectionist. They enjoy neatness and order and will organise their room in such a way that everything will have its rightful place. Books will be stacked neatly on their shelves, toys will be sorted and they will know exactly where everything is.

your Virgo child from 7 to 10 years

You have a child who takes their responsibility seriously, so entering this phase in which responsibility is the key issue can create tension. All children begin to take charge of themselves at this age and this is something your Virgo child in particular will relish. Providing them with small amounts of responsibility that they can handle well is a good way to boost their confidence.

Set your child small tasks initially that they can complete without becoming frustrated. Praise for completion and a job well done is the best reward. This is also a positive way of teaching your perfectionist Virgo child to set goals and slowly work towards them.

It is important that your child learns what is acceptable during this time and that you don't place too much responsibility on their young shoulders. They will want to make sure any task you set them is completed well, so you need to allow them time to achieve their goal. Encourage them to do their job well while at the same time teaching them that not everything requires perfection.

As Virgo children come under the influence of the planet Mercury, and earth, the cell salt that is most of use to them in times of stress is Kali Sulph (sulphate of potassium). This helps to balance the system and can be particularly useful during puberty.

your virgo teen from 11 to 14 years

As your child moves into the teen stage, they will continue to seek approval. You may find that your formerly compliant child becomes a little rebellious at this stage. Bedrooms can become a bone of contention as your formerly neat and tidy child now finds other things to occupy their mind. This stage is an interesting one in the Virgo household, as your child can appear to be undergoing a complete reversal of personality.

The child who has shown the more pedantic side of the Virgo traits now appears to be not so concerned with their appearance. Do not lose hope, as this is a stage of development that your child needs to experience. If your child leaves their room in a mess, shut the door. When they are ready, they will do the job themself and with as much fervour as they always have. The other side of the coin is that the child who has not been so concerned now begins to exhibit more of the classic Virgo characteristics, becoming the neat freak and perfectionist. Your child may also decide to become vegetarian at this stage. If that happens, don't force the issue, instead ensure that they receive all their necessary nutrients in other forms. Remember that when your child begins to challenge authority it means they are ready to take on more responsibility for themself.

When it comes to career choice, Virgos show a higher than average preference for medicine and dentistry. They also figure prominently in many of the building trades such as bricklaying, painting and metalworking. They seem to also enjoy professions such as insurance and bookkeeping but are not so highly represented in psychology, self-employment, computer-related jobs, teaching or farming. The careers they prefer reflect their ability for precision and skill in being able to focus on fine detail, areas in which they shine.

The young virgo adult

Your emerging young adult will by now have a fairly clear view of their future direction and will be able to make steady progress in achieving their goals. It is important that you encourage them to broaden their horizons, as they can become so focused on one thing that they neglect other areas of life. Encourage them to have a good balance of work and socialising and not to have their head so buried in their books that they become one-dimensional.

Your child needs a certain level of physical activity as well and if you appeal to their health-conscious side and explain how important it is for them to spend as much time on their body as their head, you should find it a relatively easy argument to win. The young Virgo is usually fairly easy to get along with, although as with all teenage boys you may find your Virgo son becomes monosyllabic for a while.

Throughout history Virgo has been assigned to the flowers buttercup, forget-me-not, aster and all nut-bearing trees. Having some of these in the garden or a picture of them in your Virgo child's room can be of benefit to them.

Famous Virgos

Agatha Christie
Richard Gere
Sean Connery
Peter Sellers
Michael Jackson
Lauren Bacall
Jack Thompson
Dawn Fraser
Sir Donald Bradman
Adam Sandler
Baz Luhrmann
William McInnes
'Dr Phil' McGraw
Salma Hayek
Charlie Sheen

Keanu Reeves
Nicole Richie
Cameron Diaz
Jack Black
Beyoncé Knowles
Teddy Geiger
Amy Winehouse
Gloria Estefan
Rupert Grint
Stephen King
Leo Tolstoy
D.H. Lawrence
Buddy Holly
Johann Wolfgang von
    Goethe

Libra child

Ruling Planet—Venus ♀
Element—Air
Quality—Cardinal
Sign—the Scales
Glyph—♎
Gemstone—Opal
Metal—Copper
22 September–23 October

'There is a garden in every childhood, an enchanted place where colours are brighter, the air softer, and the morning more fragrant than ever again.'

Elizabeth Lawrence

The Libra child is a delightful and very social little person. They are reasonably easy to care for and seem to have an in-built sense of what is socially acceptable. Your child needs peace and harmony in their surroundings and, like their symbol, the scales, they like to see balance in the world around them. They like the company of others and quite often judge themself by what they see reflected back at them in the eyes of others. Librans are generally friendly, open and generous with a ready smile. The hardest lesson for a Libran is learning to make a decision.

Your child will make an excellent arbiter in arguments, as they will always strive to be a fair and impartial judge. They can be the embodiment of tact and diplomacy and will go out of their way to avoid hurting the feelings of others.

Venus is the ruling planet affecting Libra. How it is placed in the birth horoscope will be the major influence on your child's personality and this explains why all Libra children are not the same. The Libra child with Venus in Scorpio will be a more dynamic and forceful child than the 'average' Libra, Venus in Libra adds to the need for balance and connections, while Venus in Virgo will tend to be more analytical. Venus in Leo or Sagittarius adds fire, creativity and intuition. (Venus can never be further than two signs away from the Sun, so these are the only possible positions of this planet for the Libra child.)

Venus is associated with the day Friday and the number six, so your Libra child may find them lucky.

your child's will

Your child will be a real charmer, with their sweet expression and pleasant well-balanced features. Librans are generally quite adaptable, enjoying socialising and the company of others. They are able to fit in just about anywhere quite comfortably and have the happy knack of making others feel comfortable around them. This is a trait that will show itself from quite a young age.

Libra babies are born seeking the truth; they're kind-hearted and want to be fair. They dread making mistakes or misjudgments and don't want to hurt others' feelings. Their nature compels them to seek a balanced answer before rushing into things. Where your Libra child will need the most assistance from you is in learning to express their will. Your child can be so focused on doing the right thing by everyone that they suppress their own wants and needs. Unless you want to raise a doormat, it is important that you encourage your child to stand up for themselves.

your Libra baby
from birth to 6 months

- Delightful baby, easy to please
- Charming
- Enjoys being with people and is very attentive
- Doesn't like being alone
- Needs routine
- Likes to feel comfortable

- Prefers to be held tightly, will not enjoy being 'thrown' in the air

- Soft pastel colours are best and music (such as lullabies) is an essential; and very good for settling them

Needs visual and auditory stimulation

Doesn't like too much noise or activity around them

your Libra baby

Be prepared for shopping trips to take longer than in the past, as with a Libra baby, everyone will want to stop you to admire your baby. This is a baby who seems to draw others to them; they are personable and attractive. They are not the baby who goes into a red-faced screaming and kicking rage, or creates battles at feed time. They are too well-mannered and dignified for such behaviour.

Your baby will enjoy interaction and when awake would rather be in the same room, engaging you in some form of conversation. They are not loners and even as a very young baby, your Libran will not enjoy time alone as much as time shared. Your baby will have beautiful and expressive eyes and long before they are able to communicate verbally they will use their eyes to express a gamut of emotions and needs. You will find it very easy to spend hours interacting with this delightful little bundle, and at the end of the day you will wonder where the time has gone. Babies are generally very good time-wasters for adults but this is especially true with the little Libran.

your Libra baby
from 6 to 18 months

- Becoming more and more social and will enjoy the company of other babies
- Prefers to have neatness and calm around them
- Likely to begin verbal communication quite early
- Learning all about making choices and needs time to make them
- Doesn't like to be rushed
- Prefers strong physical support
- Requires clothes that look nice but are practical and allow freedom of movement
- It is best to limit the number of toys on offer at any one time

Needs lots of hugs and to be told they are loved

Doesn't like any form of physical restriction

your Libra toddler

Your Libran toddler will begin to verbalise as early as they are able, as communication is very important to them. They will delight you for hours with their melodious babbling as they master the art of communication. Once they have, they will have an opinion on everything and wish to share that with any who will listen and even those who would prefer not to. Your child will be friendly, open and generous with smiles and chatter. Your little Libran will amaze you with their ability to mimic sounds and may drive you crazy as they cycle through their vast repertoire. This is all part of their need to be involved in whatever is going on around them. They may be difficult to get into bed as they become more aware of things around them; they don't want to miss out on something important while they are sleeping.

Try to keep the atmosphere around your child as peaceful as you can. Speak to them gently and calmly, reassuring them as much as possible. They will respond much better to your voice if you put some melody into it. They love music and will respond extremely well to you singing to them.

If you want to keep life as easy as possible for your little Libran, keep the colours in their bedroom gentle pastels and have soft music playing in the background during mealtimes and at other times when you are encouraging them to do things. Garish, loud and clashing colours can upset them emotionally, as will loud noises. Remember, your child requires peace, quiet and harmony.

Your child will follow a pattern of activity followed by inactivity. In this way they are able to stay emotionally and physically balanced.

Your little one can be so sweet and endearing that you may have difficulty not spoiling them. Remember, though, that it will be very difficult for them to adjust to school if they have had their every whim granted by their doting parents. Libran children are very resilient and don't require the amount of coddling you may think.

Libra is both musical and artistic so offer your child the opportunity to try their hand at both of these creative outlets. They will also become an avid reader as long as they are given access to books.

Your child will be extremely cooperative and more than happy to share in any work that needs to be done. They have a tendency to compare themself to others and need to learn to work at their own speed, with their own goals rather than using others as a yardstick. As their parent, keep in mind that they will put pressure on themself to try to live up to your expectations. Try to remember how important it is to them to please others and don't put any added pressure on them.

Toilet training

With the combination of the need for approval, looking good and being appreciated, the Libra child is usually very quick to learn to use the toilet. This is one child who will respond to bribery and reward systems. Night dryness may be another matter and it is quite possible that this little one will become dry during the day very early but will continue to wet the bed at night. They outgrow bed-wetting eventually and it should not become a source of contention. Praise them for their daytime dryness and encourage them be affirming that they will eventually be night-dry as well. Build them up, not down.

your Libra toddler
from 18 months to 3 years

- Desire for social interaction is increasing
- Shows concern about their appearance and begins comparing self to others
- Developing sense of values and what is and isn't fair
- Increasingly aware and curious about relationships

- Will have a stock of favourites: clothes, toys, stories, songs, etc.

Needs continual encouragement in the area of decision-making and to know that it is okay to make 'wrong' choices

Doesn't like arguments or dissent

your child's emotions

The Moon in a birth chart represents your child's emotions and instinctual responses. It is an excellent clue to how they respond in emotional situations. The Moon rules infancy and early childhood, and is the face of your child that you will see most often during the early years.

Emotions are also associated with the element water, as is the Moon. As the Moon waxes and wanes, we see the effects on the tides. It also affects all living beings. The Moon is instinctive, intuitive and empathetic. The Moon reflects the light from the Sun and is associated with similar attributes for your child. The Moon shows how your child deals with mood changes and emotions, how your child learns to become reflective and stores memories.

Your Libra Moon child will be a source of constant joy and pleasure. They will be charming and diplomatic. They will be quite affectionate, good-natured and generally popular with other people. They will have a strong need to belong and be a part of whatever is going on around them. As they adopt the attitudes and desires of those around them, they may give the appearance of being fickle. This stems from their strong need to be accepted. One of the major lessons that your little one needs to learn is that it is all right to be themself. They don't need to conform all the time in order to be accepted. People will still love them, no matter what.

Libra is represented by the scales and for your child balance is important, physically and metaphysically. The most sensitive parts of their body are their kidneys, bladder and lower back and these are the areas most likely to be affected when your child is under any form of stress.

A child with the Moon in Libra needs peace and harmony for emotional security. In order to create this peace and harmony, they may choose to compromise wherever possible. They need to learn to not be taken advantage of in this area, as their overwhelming desire for harmony could lead to their backing down in all situations. Your child needs reassurance that it is okay to stand up for themself and they don't always have to be the one to give in. They will pick up on the emotions and moods of those around them and respond accordingly, so try to minimise tension around them.

They will do their best to please you wherever possible but need time to respond to your requests. Make sure you allow them time to make up their mind if you are giving them a choice. Librans find it difficult to make hasty decisions and need time to weigh up the options.

Your child needs to withdraw for periods to recharge their batteries and settle their mind. This will be especially true if they have been through any form of emotional disturbance or where there has been a lot of activity and noise.

Libra children resonate to pastels such as lemon, pale blue, pale green, and pink, and it is indicative of their nature. They seek peace and harmony and these colours not only promote these aspects when used in clothing but are also by far the best colours to use in decorating their room.

your Libra preschooler

The character trait you are likely to find the most frustrating about your new little one as they grow is their apparent inability to make up their mind. The Libran symbol is the scales and this represents the need of a Libran to weigh up all the possibilities in any situation. This gives others the impression that they are unable or unwilling to make a decision; in actual fact they are quite capable of making decisions if given the time to do so. Your little one will not cope well, however, if they have to make a decision in a hurry and might become quite flustered in such a situation. The worst thing you can do to your little Libran is to present them with a number of different options and expect them to make a hurried choice.

Imagine this scenario at the breakfast table: they sit at the table playing with the spoon in their bowl of cereal, while at the same time toying with the slices of toast that you have prepared—just the way they like. You begin to get frustrated and tell them to hurry up and eat their breakfast; this just makes them fidget all the more. Are they hungry? Yes, they're starving. The problem is they can't make up their mind which to eat first. You have further compounded the problem by adding a cup of juice to tempt them.

Your child's preferred foods include cereals, berry fruits, apples, pears, asparagus and most fragrant spices (not hot).

It is very important with your little one to gently bring them into the world of decision-making. It is much better to present them with one thing at a time initially. They would find life much easier if you *never* presented them with a choice; unfortunately this would not prepare them for the world at large.

To help them learn to make decisions effectively it is best to offer them a limited choice until they build their confidence in this area. Instead of asking them what they would like to eat, offer them a choice of two foods that you know they enjoy and allow them time to decide which they would prefer. When selecting toys for them to play with, restrict the selection to a few toys instead of a whole boxful. The more you encourage them in this area, the greater their ability will become and as they grow in confidence they will be able to make decisions more quickly.

Also, allow them to know that it is okay to change their mind if they feel they have made a wrong choice. This may make more work for you initially as you swap their Vegemite sandwich for peanut butter or their milk for juice but if they see that a wrong choice can be corrected it will help to give them the confidence to make that decision in the first place.

- Exploring and experimenting with different social roles; behaviour will reflect this as they move from being shy and coy to outrageous and even rebellious

- Becoming more aware of the dynamics in a relationship; though they don't like confrontation, they may deliberately set up arguments between others to see what the outcome is

- Begins classifying things and people as 'better or worse than...'

- Will begin looking to others to make decisions for them and looking for someone to blame if they feel they have made a 'wrong' choice

Needs help in distinguishing the grey areas in life as well as the black and white, firm boundaries, continuing assistance with making choices

Doesn't like being rushed, too much clutter

Fun, friendship and confidence

Your child will be affectionate and will prefer company to being on their own. They will be fairly adaptable, but remember, they don't like arguments and disorder. Balance, harmony and tranquillity in the home are very important to them. They will be even-tempered and well mannered and will attract friends easily. Your child tries to be thoughtful, good-natured and go out of their way to be nice to people. You will need to watch that they don't try too hard to please other people at the expense of their own wellbeing. They may have a tendency to sacrifice their own wishes for those of others and can be taken advantage of. They may find it difficult to be assertive and stand up for themself and will need your guidance in this area.

Your child has artistic tastes and abilities and needs room to express and explore these. Give them access to music, paints, and other creative outlets. They appreciate beauty in all of its forms, whether man-made or in nature. They will see the beauty in a sunset as readily as in a Van Gogh painting or Beethoven symphony.

They need physical demonstrations of affection and like to touch and be touched. Lots of hugs and cuddles will help to keep your child happy. Music will help to soothe them when distressed. Above all, try to keep their surroundings calm and peaceful.

Libra has no animal symbol but is associated with the deer, rabbit and many birds, including the nightingale, willie wagtail and swan. These animals are all very sociable among their own but they bolt at the first sign of trouble from outsiders. Your child may enjoy a bunny or small talkative bird as a pet when they are older.

First impressions

The ascendant, or rising sign in your child's horoscope is where heaven meets Earth: the part of the sky that is visible on the horizon, looking directly to the east at the time of birth. Some say this represents the soul's entry into the earthly plane. In a birth chart it represents the physical body of an individual and shows how we meet the world head-on. It is referred to as the mask we wear when we first meet people, the filter through which all of the planets within the birth chart are expressed.

With Libra on the ascendant, your child is certain to be sweet and charming. They will have a pleasant face and may have a dimple. They will be a little on the fair side, within the realms of the family colouring. Once again within the family characteristics, they will have an attractive face with large, beautiful eyes and a lovely smile. They are likely to be a little below average height with a long body in proportion to their legs. Their disposition will be gentle and accommodating.

Your child will be charming and friendly with a genuine interest in others. They are pleasant and gentle, and as they grow you will find them easy to talk to and get along with. Your child may be a little superficial at times, judging people by their appearance or status, rather than who they really are.

They will want to please everyone in everything they do. Your child likes peace and harmony and dislikes loud noise and arguments. They are gracious and sociable and have a strong sense of fair play. They will seek to find balance and justice in the world and have a tendency to take the side of the underdog. Capable of seeing both sides in any situation, they may appear to be indecisive at times, as they weigh up their options.

Your child will be good at debating but is not argumentative. They enjoy a good discussion and playing with words. They would probably make a good lawyer or politician.

your Libra child
from 7 to 10 years

This is the beginning of the development of responsibility. Your Libra child should have little trouble with this phase of growing up. They will take any responsibility you give them quite seriously, but remember to allocate them one task at a time if you want them to succeed.

Provide them with small tasks initially that they can complete without becoming confused, and provide a suitable reward scheme. A daily star chart, which has a larger reward when a certain number of stars is reached, can be ideal. Your child is now also developing an awareness of money and material possessions, so providing them with pocket money in return for chores they've completed can work quite well on a number of levels. Your child will also begin to understand laws and democracy at this age, so including them in the setting of rules and punishments can be a good idea.

As Libra children come under the influence of the planet Venus, the cell salt that is most of use to them in times of stress is Nat Phos (sodium phosphate). This is useful in rebalancing the system and can be particularly beneficial during puberty.

your Libra teen
from 11 to 14 years

As your Libran moves from child to teen, they are usually reasonably calm. Your child will generally be keen to follow the rules and behave in an appropriate fashion. They can, however, have occasional outbursts as they try to be more self-assertive. This is not an easy task for them and so it can be expressed inappropriately at first. Guide them as to how to be heard without the need to shout.

Your child will become quite social and may need reminding of their commitments, such as homework and chores. They will need firm guidelines and these must be consistent: if the rule is no outings unless homework is done, then this needs to be enforced, no matter the occasion. Help your child become responsible by being a responsible parent.

As far as career choices go, it is no surprise that Librans rank way over average in law studies. They also have a higher than average showing in bricklaying, painting and hairdressing. Librans appear able to adapt to most careers but enjoy those where they can express themselves, either creatively or through their use of argument and reason. Statistics also show that Librans are not so keen on teaching, farming, dentistry or medicine.

The young Libra adult

Your young Libra adult will become more social the older they get. Dating will become very important to them and they will be keen not to be without a boyfriend/girlfriend. They are generally fairly law-abiding and aren't likely to get into too much trouble. Rules are still important and having a curfew until they are older is probably a good idea.

You need to encourage your emerging Libra adult to be responsible for themself. This means not just keeping to the rules, but also taking care of some of their own basic needs such as making their bed, doing their own laundry and helping with cooking meals. They can be so busy that if you allow it, your house can become just a stopover, where they call in to sleep and pick up clean clothes. This is not being personally responsible and you need to show them your love by not doing so much for them.

Their natural eye for beauty and harmony means that Librans are attracted to the more visually appealing and scented plants, such as rose, dahlia, daisy, lilac, ash, poplar and apple tree plants.

Famous Libras

Julie Andrews
Brigitte Bardot
Charlie Brown
Dwight Eisenhower
T.S. Eliot
Mahatma Gandhi
George Gershwin
Charlton Heston
Deborah Kerr
Samuel Coleridge
Eugene O'Neill
Oscar Wilde
John Lennon

Franz Liszt
Will Smith
Matt Damon
Hugh Jackman
Richard Harris
Naomi Watts
Kate Winslet
Ashlee Simpson
Alicia Silverstone
Avril Lavigne
Eminem
Gwen Stefani
Olivia Newton-John

scorpio child

Ruling Planet—Mars ♂
Element—Water
Quality—Fixed
Sign—the Scorpion
Glyph—♏
Gemstone—Topaz, malachite
Metal—Iron, steel
23 October–21 November

'Your vision will become clear only when you look into your heart. Who looks outside, dreams. Who looks inside, awakens.'
Carl Jung

Scorpios are intense, deep and complex. They are attentive and sensitive and can be withdrawn. They need privacy and periodical 'time out'. They can have an intense gaze that you know is burning right through to your very soul. Strong and determined, both physically and mentally, they see life as a challenge to meet full-on.

You will notice from the beginning how serious and attentive this little one is. They will sleep quite well but when they are awake, you will be amazed at how intently they take everything in. They are extremely sensitive to all that goes on around them. They will know how you are feeling and will respond accordingly. They may not smile very often but when they do you know they mean it. To be on the receiving end of this little one's grin is a wonderful experience, as when they smile they do so with their whole self.

Mars is the ruling planet affecting Scorpio. How it is placed in the birth horoscope will be the major influence on your child's personality and this explains why all Scorpio children are not the same. The Scorpio child with Mars in Pisces, Cancer or Scorpio will be much more sensitive than the 'average' Scorpio, Mars in Gemini, Libra or Aquarius will tend to be more of a chatterbox, Mars in Capricorn, Taurus or Virgo will be more grounded and directed, while Mars in Aries, Leo or Sagittarius will be very active.

Mars is also associated with the day Tuesday, and the number nine, so your Scorpio child may find them lucky.

your child's will

Scorpio seems to have an in-built reflector that mirrors back an image of whatever the child perceives around them. This can produce some quite extreme behaviour from your little Scorpio. If you are very talkative, they may prefer to communicate non-verbally; if you are very sporty, they may exhibit a lack of interest in sport but excel in art or music. If there are siblings in the family, watch your Scorpio child manifest opposite behaviour traits to their siblings.

As noted earlier, this is a very complex child—so complex that for a long time they won't understand themself. If you ask them why they have done something, their answer is likely to be, 'I don't know'. In truth, they don't. It does seem that they have a mandate to be contrary and make life's lessons difficult for themself. They are very determined and have a strong will. This can be to their own detriment, especially when they dig their heels in and refuse to budge. Reverse psychology works well with your Scorpio child and is a much better strategy than locking horns.

your scorpio baby from birth to 6 months

- Serious and intense
- Cautious and self-contained
- Likes routine and doesn't like surprises
- Needs affection and cuddles, but on their own terms
- Needs to feel safe and protected
- Doesn't like to feel controlled or shamed
- Won't 'perform' on demand

Needs unconditional love

Doesn't like to be tickled

your scorpio baby

Your baby will not be particularly cuddly but will enjoy regular close contact. Your child will dictate how much physical contact they have—when and for how long. When they have had enough they will pull away and you will have no doubt as to their intent. Your child's strong will and determination will be obvious even as an infant.

Your baby will be relatively easy when it comes to feeding and sleeping and will respond well to massage with gently scented oils such as lavender and chamomile. You will find when your baby is awake, they will be wide awake, alert and taking in everything that is going on around them. Your baby is best settled in a quiet room on their own, as although they will be a relatively good sleeper they can have trouble getting to sleep if there are any distractions. Bathtime will be a source of pleasure for both baby and parent.

your scorpio baby from 6 to 18 months

- Continues to be intense and serious
- Becoming aware of their surroundings and looking to understand how things work (particularly people)
- Begins to exhibit behaviour aimed solely at gaining a reaction

- Enjoys water play
- Likes games that involve fitting shapes, colours, etc. together
- Begins to discover fun things that others find distasteful, such as playing in mud or, better yet, what is in their nappy
- Enjoys tactile play such as finger-painting, play dough or mud pies

Needs approval and permission to get dirty, time alone and space

Doesn't like discipline or being laughed at, even at this tender age

your Scorpio toddler

Your Scorpio toddler is very vulnerable and, being sensitive, picks up on everything. As a result they will employ self-protection measures to block out negative energy they may encounter. This protective behaviour can range from trying to placate those they feel are in distress to total withdrawal from a situation or person they find overwhelming.

Your child will be like an immovable object once they have set their mind to something. They will be the most determined child you are likely to meet. This is one trait that will not ease off as they grow but will be very useful for them once they learn to control their strong will. They will have the ability to follow even the toughest course through to the end, no matter what obstacles arise.

Even though it will be on their terms, your child needs physical contact and signs of affection, as long as it is not too stifling. They are physically tough and may not let you know if they are feeling unwell until it reaches crisis point.

You may find it difficult to know what your Scorpio child wants at times and this may lead to some amount of frustration for each of you. The problem is quite often that they don't know what they do want, they only know what they *don't* want. Your child needs to go through the options and only by rejecting those they know aren't right do they discover what *is* right. This is a very important process for them, as while they are sorting through these choices they are, learning who they are as opposed to who they are not. If they are ever to soar like the eagle, they must learn that this is as much a part of who they are as the stinging scorpion.

They will prefer their surroundings to be peaceful, clean, and attractive and would probably be happier in a bedroom with an older-style setting rather than modern furniture. They will take great pleasure spending time in the garden and appreciate the beauty of nature. They will also enjoy trips to the beach and could be a very good swimmer, just like fellow Scorpio Aleksandr Popov, the Olympic freestyle gold medallist.

Your Scorpio child may be quite artistic, with a good eye for detail and a strong sense of touch. They will enjoy creating things from clay (initially playdough), working with wood, and they will certainly enjoy finger-painting. Once they become engrossed in something they will not like being interrupted, preferring to work slowly and thoroughly.

It is said that the eyes are the windows to the soul and you will find this is especially true with your Scorpio child. If you are ever in doubt as to what they are feeling or thinking, look into their eyes; they may be able to hide their feelings elsewhere but it will always show in their eyes.

Your child will be very good at weighing people up on first meeting and their instincts will be very strong. Although you may find it hard to understand them at times and know what they are thinking or feeling, the reverse is certainly not true, as they will very quickly know what you are feeling and thinking. One of the worst things you can do with your little Scorpio is to lie to them or hide the truth. They can deal with just about any situation in life, as long as you are honest with them. They will resent evasiveness, as they will already know when something is wrong. This is evident almost from birth.

With your Scorpio child, everything is either black or white, there is no such thing as grey. They will be strong-willed and determined and will always maintain a facade of being calm and in control, even if they are a bowl of jelly on the inside.

Toilet training

Toilet training can become a battleground if not handled carefully. The Scorpio child has a fascination with the body and bodily functions and the manner in which toilet training is handled can determine how the child will feel about these things as they grow. Parents can make things easier by accepting their child's interest and not being repelled or showing disgust. The result will usually be that their little

Scorpio is likely to just do it all themself with the appropriate explanations and encouragement. Do not shame them at all or try to force or coerce them in any way, as this will cause them to feel shame about their body and set up a power struggle where no one wins. Give them encouragement and show patience and remember their great need for privacy and things will go relatively smoothly.

your Scorpio toddler from 18 months to 3 years

- Increasingly sensitive
- May appear sulky but is showing an increased need for privacy
- Can be a late talker, as Scorpios prefer to wait until they have something to say
- Will begin to test their power and the boundaries
- Can become stubborn and rebellious and the word 'no' may seem like the only word this child knows
- The term 'terrible twos' was probably coined by the parent of a Scorpio toddler
- May ask awkward questions about sex and death

Needs honest but age appropriate answers to questions

Doesn't like not knowing

your child's emotions

The Moon in a birth chart represents your child's emotions and instinctual responses. It is an excellent clue to how they respond in emotional situations. The Moon rules infancy and early childhood, and is the face of your child that you will see most often during the early years.

Emotions are also associated with the element water, as is the Moon. As the Moon waxes and wanes, we see the effects on the tides. It also affects all living beings. The Moon is instinctive, intuitive and empathetic. The Moon reflects the light from the Sun and is associated with similar attributes for your child. The Moon shows how your child deals with mood changes and emotions, how your child learns to become reflective and stores memories.

You have in your care a very special little soul, who will be intense and passionate with deep feelings. They will be quite emotional and extremely sensitive; still waters run deep, and so it is with your Scorpio child. There will be a tendency to keep their true feelings to themself, which is their way of protecting themself emotionally.

The body parts most susceptible for Scorpio are the bladder and genitals. These areas of the body are most likely to show problems in times of stress.

Your child will have an amazing memory, which also means they will not easily forget hurts. Their intuition is strong and they will rely on this a lot when they are exposed to new people. Although they may appear quick to judge, their first instincts are usually proved correct.

If they are hurt emotionally or rejected it is unlikely that the person responsible will be given a second chance. Your Scorpio child's emotions can be so powerful they can be overwhelming.

Your child will benefit greatly if you are able to help them to be more rational when dealing with emotional situations.

Scorpio children resonate to dark red, maroon and smoky greys. As they have a tendency to be broody it would be a good idea to include some brighter colours in the scheme of their room. In particular, vibrant yellows, blues and greens will help.

your Scorpio preschooler

As a preschooler the Scorpio child continues to exhibit intensity and volatility. Their fears are beginning to surface now and one of the things they fear the most is fear itself. They will not like you to notice they are afraid of anything but at the same time need your reassurance. This can be a difficult time for both parent and child: your child really needs to know that they are loved and while they will relish the comfort of a hug, they will not seek it and may in fact try to push you away. They need to be hugged in an appropriate way for them, so hold them for as long as they will tolerate and then release them as soon as they have had enough. This will give them the reassurance they need while still allowing them to be in control.

Your child will continue to push and test the boundaries and what they are looking for is the reassurance that there is an adult in charge. Patience and perseverance are key words for parents at this stage. Your child needs rules and discipline; rules that are fair and designed to keep them safe, and discipline that is reasonable. The Scorpio sense of justice is one of the most developed in a child and determines the way they judge the world.

> Your child's Mars connection creates an affinity with foods such as leeks, shallots and most pungent and sharp-tasting foods. You may find it useful to include small amounts of these in the diet once your child's palate is mature enough to appreciate them.

It is also important at this stage to not become 'caught up' in the child's drama. Keep a cool head when reacting to any scene that the child is creating. If you pass the Scorpio child's continual testing then you will be rewarded with their sweet and loving side. If you fail and the child feels that you are not in control, they will continue to push.

They need, above all, to feel loved and accepted for themself, no matter what they try. They can be impatient, a little on the moody side and are likely to brood if they feel they have been unjustly treated.

Your child will be very determined, achieving whatever they set their mind to. They will be constantly searching for new challenges, new problems to solve and new mountains to climb. Your child will recover quickly from illness, disappointments and in extreme cases even from death's door. As a result, they may think they are invincible and this can lead them into trouble, as they are prone to take risks and seem to have very little sense of danger.

As they tend to hide their true feelings, they will bottle up their anger, which can result in sudden outbursts. Some form of physical activity would be very beneficial in helping to burn off their excess emotional energy. They can be very possessive toward those they love and this can lead to jealousy if they feel someone is encroaching on their territory.

Your preschooler is a paradoxical child who on one hand seeks challenge and excitement and on the other security and comfort. They are able to read other people very clearly but keep their own feelings hidden from others. They are intense, tenacious and capable, with a tendency to be stubborn on occasion.

your scorpio preschooler from 3 to 6 years

- Can become quite volatile
- Can be extremely sensitive
- Requires lots of honest explanation but will bristle at being lectured
- Requires physical activity; a good age to introduce organised and team sports
- Beginning to grasp the concept of consequences of actions but will require the assistance of adults in this area for a long while yet
- Will continue to push and test the boundaries

Needs your reassurance, explanations, rules and discipline, honesty

Doesn't like lectures, rejection, humiliation

Fun, friendship and confidence

Your child will be extremely loyal and make a great confidante, as they are very good at keeping secrets. Your child will have a small circle of close and trusted friends. Scorpios are slow to form friendships, but once made, these will be treasured.

They can have a tendency to suffer from low self-esteem and if you want to boost their confidence you need to be sincere and consistent; praise them often, but mean it. They will see right through insincerity and this will only make them doubt even more.

Praise them whenever they do something truly deserving of praise but give them plenty of support and love at all times. They will need more love, nurturing, support and reassurance than other children but the extra effort will be returned tenfold. They require firm but gentle discipline; above all, it must be fair. Your child will have very definite ideas about what is fair and what isn't. If you want their respect you must earn it and you will not earn their respect if you are inconsistent. They admire strength of character and respect those they see as being strong of mind and will.

Your little Scorpio will enjoy outdoor activities and is quite a physical child. They need to burn off their excess energy and will enjoy swimming and athletics. This sort of activity needs to be balanced with time spent on quiet tasks such as reading and playing indoor games, even exploring their creative talents, of which there will be many.

Your child needs firm boundaries and you need to stick to the rules once they are made. You cannot allow them to do something one day and not the next, or vice versa. If you don't want them to jump on other people's furniture, then don't allow them to do it at home. If meals are to be eaten at the table, everyone should eat at the table, all the time. This child needs to know what the rules are and to see everyone abiding by them. Try to keep the rules simple and clear, and apply them consistently.

There are a number of animal symbols associated with the sign of Scorpio, reflecting the complexity of their nature. The scorpion is representative of the tendency to be their own worst enemy with their stubbornness, but is just one face of your child. The panther, hawk, owl and eagle are also associated with this sign, as is the legendary phoenix. Mostly they are representative of the heights to which your child can soar once they harness their determination. Watch them rise from the ashes and soar like the eagle.

First impressions

The ascendant, or rising sign in your child's horoscope is where heaven meets Earth: the part of the sky that is visible on the horizon, looking directly to the east at the time of birth. Some say this represents the soul's entry into the earthly plane. In a birth chart it represents the physical body of an individual and shows how we meet the world head-on. It is referred to as the mask we wear when we first meet people. The filter through which all of the planets within the birth chart are expressed.

Your child will have a piercing gaze that you will swear allows them to see right into the heart and soul of others. Scorpio on the ascendant adds incredible intensity to the gaze and the eyes are one of Scorpio's most notable physical characteristics—not for their colour or beauty, although both of these things are also present, but for their depth. Many people are put off by the gaze of a Scorpio and can feel intimidated by it.

Your child will have an added cautiousness, be reserved and possibly even a little withdrawn at times. They will try to hide their true feelings and emotions and will be great at putting on a 'poker face'. Don't make the mistake of interpreting this as 'I don't care', as nothing could be further from the truth. This is a deeply caring child but one who also feels vulnerable and therefore prefers to keep their feelings to themself. The symbol for Scorpio is the scorpion, and just like this tough little desert creature your child will present a hard shell to the outside world.

They are, underneath the hard exterior, gentle and easily hurt—and slow to forget. As it develops, their personality will be intense and magnetic and people will be attracted by their charm. Your child will be tough and determined and once they set their mind to something, they will become immovable until they have completed their task or reached their goal.

> Your child will need you to respect their privacy and to give them your trust. Even from a very young age they will become quite upset if they feel their privacy has been invaded.

your Scorpio child from 7 to 10 years

Your child is now at the age where they are developing a sense of responsibility. This can be a time that creates both fear and pride in your child. They will take pride in achieving the goals you set but at the same time fear losing your ongoing care if they prove to be too capable. As ever with this child, reassurance is the key factor.

Your child has a magnetic personality and they can become very good at using this to manipulate situations to their advantage. At this stage in their development it is important that they learn to take on responsibility for themself. Your child will continue to be very private and keep their feelings and emotions tightly hidden. They may appear unresponsive to situations but don't be fooled by their cool exterior; this child feels deeply. They will often not show their true feelings, for fear of exposing their vulnerability to others, who will gain power over them.

Your child can be blunt and may develop sarcasm at this age; they are very forthright and will not suffer fools lightly. This can be a good time to instil a little diplomacy into your child's kit bag.

As Scorpio children come under the influence of the water side of the planet Mars, the cell salt that is most of use to them in times of stress is Calc Sulph (calcium sulphate). This helps in rebalancing the system and can be particularly useful during puberty.

your scorpio teen from 11 to 14 years

Your Scorpio teen can become quite rebellious throughout this stage and will certainly begin to challenge those in positions of authority. Although they will keep their own thoughts and feelings concealed, they will know what everyone around them is thinking and feeling. Remember, they are highly sensitive and tuned in to their surroundings. It is best to be forthright and honest with them; if they ask questions, no matter how awkward, answer honestly.

Don't try to mollycoddle them. They can cope with just about anything, if you are honest. If they sense you are upset they will try to ease your pain. This child who very rarely openly displays affection is likely to sidle up and give you a hug or just a touch of their hand, to let you know that they are there.

Your Scorpio teen will not be one to create a fuss over things and will try to take care of situations themself wherever possible. They feel that if something is their responsibility, it is up to them to take care of it, and they are highly unlikely to ask for help or advice. You need to openly discuss matters such as sex, alcohol and drugs with your child as they are likely to experiment and need to be informed of the dangers. Again, do this with openness and honesty and don't try scare tactics, as with this child it is likely to make the prospect sound even more tantalising.

Perhaps it is due to the fact that Scorpios spend their life observing the undercurrents, but when it comes to career choices, even though they would appear ideally suited, Scorpio ranks low among psychology students. They are also not overly interested in management, teaching or journalism. Where they do rank highly is among bakers, tailors, bricklayers, painters, carpenters, computer programmers and hairdressers. Most of these professions work well with the Scorpio need to be physical and be alone with their thoughts.

The young Scorpio adult

Your young Scorpio can become broody as they move into adulthood. They will continue to explore the undercurrents of life and can become quite secretive, to the eyes of a parent. It is important to remember at this stage that your Scorpio has always valued their privacy. It doesn't mean they are hiding anything, they are just being true to their character. Your young adult will continue to be fascinated by life and death and all that is in between. Black will be the preferred colour and whatever is the latest 'underground' music will be their favourite.

They will enjoy seeing the reaction of adults to their behaviour and the best way to deal with your child at this stage is to be as non-reactive as possible. Accept it as another 'stage' they are going through. As always, your child is looking for your approval, no matter what. That is their charter in life: to challenge and still find acceptance.

You need to continue to keep firm boundaries—which your child will continue to push—and fair but enforced rules. Keep the communication open but respect your child's privacy and don't push.

Throughout history, like Aries, Scorpio has been assigned to thorn-bearing trees, and flowers such as chrysanthemum, honeysuckle and gentian. Having these in the garden or even a picture of them in the house can bring enjoyment to Scorpio.

Famous Scorpios

Bram Stoker
Goldie Hawn
Jodie Foster
John Cleese
Prince Charles
Charles Bronson
John Singleton
Joan Sutherland
Helen Reddy
Julia Roberts

Owen Wilson
Keith Urban
Leonardo DiCaprio
Delta Goodrem
Meg Ryan
Ellen Pompeo
Anne Hathaway
k.d. lang
Pink
Bill Gates

Sagittarius child

Ruling Planet—Jupiter ♃
Element—Fire
Quality—Mutable
Sign—the Archer
Glyph—♐
Gemstone—Turquoise
Metal—Tin
21 November–21 December

'There is always one moment in childhood when
the door opens and lets the future in.'

Deepak Chopra

Sagittarius is the fire sign of Jupiter and those born under this sign are warm and loving, adventurous and inquisitive. The Sagittarian child is outgoing, bright and sunny and loves to learn and discover. Your child can in turn be sullen and introverted and even a little depressed at times, usually as a result of their light and wit shining a little too brightly, leading to a 'burnout'. During these times the little Sag needs those around them to be the bright light for a while and allow them to rekindle their fire. Generally the life of any party or family/social gathering, they are natural entertainers. These children can be the bane of a teacher's life and generally take on the role of 'class clown'.

Jupiter is the ruling planet affecting Sagittarius. How it is placed in the birth horoscope will be the major influence on your child's personality and this explains why all Sagittarius children are not the same. The Sagittarius child with Jupiter in Pisces will be much more sensitive than the 'average' Sagittarius, whereas Aries, Leo and Sagittarius can be adventurous, even reckless. Jupiter in Cancer will tend to be more family and home oriented, while Jupiter in Capricorn, Taurus or Virgo will be more grounded and directed. The child with a Scorpio Jupiter can be serious, while in Gemini, Libra or Aquarius more curious.

Jupiter is also associated with the day Thursday, and the number three, so your Sagittarius child may find them lucky.

your child's will

Your Sagittarius child will fill your life with fun and laughter. They will be a bright, inquisitive and adventurous little spirit. They will be happy and playful, in fact a miniature clown, who will keep themselves and all those around them amused with their antics and wonderful sense of fun.

If you are at all familiar with the character Huckleberry Finn, you have some idea of the nature of your Sagittarius child. Mark Twain was a Sagittarian and his nature is reflected in his best known and loved stories. Sagittarians have a somewhat wanderlust nature and desire for adventure. If you can, picture Huck Finn, with his cut-off jeans and his homemade fishing pole slung over his shoulder, heading off into the woods to seek adventure. This is a fitting image for the little Sagittarian, no matter whether boy or girl.

While not so much a determined child, your child does need space and freedom to explore the world around them and can become morose if these aren't available. They can be quite scattered with their energy and need direction and firm boundaries.

your Sagittarius baby from birth to 6 months

- Alert and cheerful
- Squirmy and restless
- Either sleeping or in perpetual motion
- Happy and playful
- Needs the company of others

- May cry if left alone
- Will sleep better if in a room where they can hear familiar voices
- Enjoys storytelling and will benefit even at this earliest stage from being read stories

Needs plenty of fresh air, sunshine and freedom to move around

Doesn't like being confined, ignored or left alone for too long

your Sagittarius baby

Your baby will be alert and cheerful, although restless. Your child will be either sleeping or in perpetual motion. Placid and calm are not words used often when describing a Sagittarian. Even as a very small baby, they will show their sunny disposition and their desire for companionship. It is likely that they will cry if left on their own; however, if you move their cradle into the room where everyone else is, they are likely to sleep contentedly, as they listen to the comforting sound of familiar voices. If you find this is the case and want them to sleep in their own room, try leaving a radio switched on, tuned to a talkback station.

If they become unsettled, taking them for a walk outside may help. As they are a freedom-loving child, they will settle better if not wrapped too tightly when put into bed. If you are worried about them getting a chill when the weather is cooler, a little sleeping bag may be the best suggestion, as they will try to kick their blankets off. Generally they are a happy baby but can be a restless and fitful sleeper.

- Curious and needs to be supervised around flames, developing a fascination with fire at this age
- Enjoys travelling away from home
- Curious and willing to learn new skills
- Loves listening to stories; is already developing a wonderful imagination
- Enjoys a variety of physical activities; would do well at 'kindy gym' or something similar

Needs to develop the distinction between reality and fantasy, lots of laughter, freedom to move around and explore under supervision

Doesn't like restriction or being stifled

your Sagittarius toddler

One of the first words your child is likely to utter will be 'why'. Be prepared for the onslaught, as every request you make of them will be followed with 'why'. They will wake with a question on their lips and fall asleep with another forming in their mind. Your child can drive you to the point of distraction, until in desperation you turn around and tell them, 'If you ask me "why" one more time I am going to go crazy'. Their response will be 'But why?' So be prepared— they're not being perverse, they really do have an insatiable curiosity about the world.

Your child can also have difficulty in accepting or coping with disappointment. It goes against their nature to accept defeat, or to admit that they have made a wrong choice, or to simply accept that sometimes life is hard. Their belief in the positive side of life can be so firmly entrenched that they simply refuse to see the more negative aspects of the real world. This can lead to them responding to stress or upset in ways that may seem inappropriate.

Your child is very easygoing and adaptable. They will enjoy listening to tall stories and mythical adventures and as soon as they are old enough will begin reading themself.

Your child needs freedom and room to explore and will need to be watched, as they are the kind of child who will wander off in a shopping centre. They are also likely to disappear from home and you may find them down the street visiting the neighbours. You will need to instil in them that they are not to wander off without you and not to talk to strangers. As they are so friendly, and at the same time naive, they have no sense of danger where people are concerned.

They will need space within the home as well as outside and may have difficulties with boundaries, which makes it even more important that you set some from an early age.

Your little Sagittarian is likely to be an early walker, and be into everything. Remember, your child learns through experience and therefore needs to explore and expand their horizons to gain this experience. Nevertheless, they do need supervision and safe areas to explore, along with boundaries, to keep them secure. I am sure that the phrase 'curiosity killed the cat' was first uttered by the parent of a small Sagittarian.

They will be generous with their playmates and usually quite willing to share their toys. Very rarely will there be arguments over possessions with your toddler. They will be very energetic and will benefit from regular naps during the day.

Your Sagittarius child will be charming, warm and friendly with a wonderful sense of fun and joy for life. They will be an optimistic child, with a delightful, if somewhat quirky, sense of humour.

Toilet training

Toilet training is usually an erratic process, fabulous one day with the next full of 'accidents'. This child does not respond to external motivation; their motivation for everything in life comes from within. No amount of bribery or cajoling will make the process any easier. They want to please, however, and if gently guided with lots of patience will eventually get it right all by themself, in their own time.

your Sagittarius toddler from 18 months to 3 years

- Becoming more outgoing and independent
- Playful, brave and reckless
- Curious and inquisitive
- Discovers the word 'why' and expects the answers
- Becomes curious about God and religion
- Beginning to develop their idealism
- Can become rebellious and is eager to try new things
- Very creative with a rich fantasy life
- Can be very untidy as there are too many things waiting to be discovered to worry about tidying up the mess created along the way

Needs Short answers to the continual questions, quiet times, encouragement in their discovery, interesting excursions, security and firm boundaries and rules

Doesn't like feeling lost, restriction or being forced to do anything

your child's emotions

The Moon in a birth chart represents your child's emotions and instinctual responses. It is an excellent clue to how they respond in emotional situations. The Moon rules infancy and early childhood, and is the face of your child that you will see most often during the early years.

Emotions are also associated with the element water, as is the Moon. As the Moon waxes and wanes, we see the effects on the tides. It also affects all living beings. The Moon is instinctive, intuitive and empathetic. The Moon reflects the light from the Sun and is associated with similar attributes for your child. The Moon shows how your child deals with mood changes and emotions, how your child learns to become reflective and stores memories.

Your Sagittarius child will be warm, cheerful and outgoing. They have an in-built sense of fun and adventure and the biggest problem you may have with them will be keeping them still.

They can be restless as they're mentally and physically active. They will require a large amount of physical activity to help burn off their excess energy. They will be constantly wandering, if not physically, at least in their head.

Your Sagittarius child will keep you constantly amused with their antics. They can be a real clown and nothing gives them greater pleasure than to see you smile and hear you laugh.

Your child tends to go into situations without thinking and can be accident-prone. The thighs and buttocks are the most vulnerable part of the body for your Sagittarius child, which can be partly to do with their tripping over their own feet.

Your child is emotionally resilient, although they can be prone to darker moods and will brood at times. This is rare, as they usually keep their darker emotions to themself, preferring to put on a happy face for others. It is important that you encourage your child to share their feelings and to let them know that it is okay to be sad sometimes. Teaching your child to embrace their emotions when young may help prevent the development of depression when they are older.

They may tend to overindulge in food, so it is a good thing that their natural tendency is to be physically active, otherwise they could develop a problem with their weight. They will tackle everything they do in life with enthusiasm and optimism. They see the silver lining in every cloud and don't understand the meaning of 'can't'. They believe there is always a solution to every problem, if they just keep looking.

Sagittarius children resonate to the colours dark blue, purple and violet and these colours can help soothe them. Incorporate these colours into the colour scheme of your child's room and their clothing. It is also helpful for them to have some yellow and orange to help boost them in times of lower vitality.

your Sagittarius preschooler

Your child will have a broad and expansive mind but may lack the ability to focus and concentrate on detailed tasks. They will need your assistance to develop this skill. On the other hand, they will have an amazing ability to sort through huge amounts of information and see patterns and meanings that are beyond the capabilities of most others to see.

They will think metaphorically, symbolically, mythically and ironically, rather than literally. This gives them the ability to be a wonderful storyteller. Your child will have a vivid imagination and is able to see things from a totally different perspective to most. They will love to share their adventures and the new things they have learnt, whether you want to hear them or not. They may need assistance in understanding the difference between a good story and a lie.

Overall, your child will enjoy learning and should have no difficulties once it comes time to start school, although a few lessons in tact and diplomacy while they are still very young may avoid some difficulties as they grow. Remember their implicit honesty: they are likely to point out to their teacher that they have bad breath, or a moustache, something they may well be aware of but would prefer not have announced in front of the entire class. While their honesty is admirable and endearing, they will need to learn that sometimes honesty is not the best policy.

Still, they should enjoy school; their great curiosity makes learning a pleasure. If you find this is not the case you need to go to school and find out why, as a bad introduction to formal learning for this child can lead to lifetime problems. They may have difficulty with strict rules, or a dull and boring teacher. As they are naturally restless they may also have difficulty in sitting still and being quiet for long periods.

Your Sagittarius child will have an affinity with bulb vegetables, such as carrots, beets and turnips; also onion, leek and celery; and fruit and berries such as currants, sultanas and mulberries. It is quite possible that they will not be big meat-eaters, especially red meat, so include plenty of healthy vegetables that they will enjoy in their diet.

They may have a tendency to speak before thinking and could suffer a little from foot-in-mouth disease but if you treat them with trust they will respond with honesty. You will find that the honour system will work well with them, as they are unlikely to cheat or lie, as long as they are trusted. If you don't treat them with trust, they may take the attitude that if they are not believed anyway, then why bother trying.

Your child can accept any explanation you give them as long as it is genuine. Do not try to pull the wool over this child's eyes. If you're fair and honest with them, they will develop respect for both you and your rules. If on the other hand you are unfair, unjust or are making demands on them for the sake of your own peace and quiet, you will be met with obstinacy.

Your preschooler will really enjoy any outdoor activity, but particularly hiking, bushwalking, bike-riding or even skiing. They will probably show an interest in foreign lands and cultures from an early age and will be very curious about how other people live. They will love learning and sharing their knowledge with others. This is the sort of little child who, when they come home from school, will tell you everything they learnt that day.

your Sagittarius preschooler from 3 to 6 years

- Attention span can be short with a need for variety
- Extremely restless and curious
- May have difficulty differentiating between reality and fantasy
- Daydreams and becomes very good at storytelling
- Their natural charm and friendliness makes it easy to make new friends
- Their curiosity and keenness to learn make the early years of schooling easy, fun and exciting
- Likely to have imaginary friends who take part in their fantasy life

Needs honesty, distinction between real and fantasy, information, understanding, explanations and to learn restraint

Doesn't like lack of boundaries and structure, overprotection, feeling deprived or not being allowed to grow up

Fun, friendship and confidence

Your child should have no difficulty in making friends, as their natural exuberance and sense of fun will make them quite popular with their peers. These same qualities, however, mixed with their sense of larrikinism may find them getting into difficulties with their teachers. They love meeting new people and are very open and friendly but they can be naive.

Your child needs space and freedom to move around and explore. If you live in an apartment or small townhouse, try to take them to the local park as often as possible. They will enjoy visiting people and exchanging ideas and opinions. They are likely to be interested in other cultures and in different religions, examining alternative ways of experiencing life.

Your young Sagittarian will be fairly adaptable and would rather forgive than bear a grudge. They will notice the differences in people rather than the similarities, as they are more interested in how people who are different can still connect on some level. They are likely to show interest in many different things and could go through quite a few 'fads' before they actually find what really interests them.

Their optimism may get them into trouble occasionally as they grow. They are very outgoing and have a sense of invincibility regarding their own personal safety. They will try just about anything but tend not to think of the possible dangers. They are likely to walk up to a snarling dog with their hand outstretched to pat it, believing that the dog will roll over wagging his tail just like their puppy at home.

Their mental attitude is very similar, in that they are not afraid to tackle anything if it interests them. They will enjoy learning and for the most part find it challenging and fun. They will be popular at school, as they are warm, funny and intelligent, and accept people for who they are.

The symbol for Sagittarius is the centaur, and like their mythical counterpart they are constantly 'on the go'. The centaur also represents their ability to see far and to aim their ambitions high. They also have an affinity with horse, deer and hunted animals and make good conservationists and animal rights campaigners.

First impressions

The ascendant, or rising sign in your child's horoscope is where heaven meets Earth: the part of the sky that is visible on the horizon, looking directly to the east at the time of birth. Some say this represents the soul's entry into the earthly plane. In a birth chart it represents the physical body of an individual and shows how we meet the world head-on. It is referred to as the mask we wear when we first meet people. The filter through which all of the planets within the birth chart are expressed.

With Sagittarius on the ascendant, your child will be on the slim side when young, and long and rangy. The thighs are generally long and well developed. They will have a slightly elongated face, with a strong jaw line. Their teeth should be white and straight, with a wide sparkling smile. They will have attractive eyes and hair.

They will be outwardly friendly, carefree and cheerful. They are quite happy when meeting new people and very rarely shy. They will be blunt and to the point and may lack a little in the tact and diplomacy area, but will never deliberately say or do anything to be hurtful.

They will be naturally curious about people and places and are likely to travel when they grow a little older. They love interacting with people and exchanging information and ideas. Your child will have a wonderful sense of humour, and this can be obvious from a very young age as they giggle and chortle to themself in private jokes. They will be warm and loving and want to share their warmth with those around them.

Your child will be a natural teacher as they share their knowledge with others. They will have an interest in philosophy, religion and spiritual matters, as this fits with their natural curiosity about people and the way they think and live.

They will enjoy outdoor activities and would prefer to spend part of the day outside in the fresh air. They may not necessarily be sporty but will enjoy physical activity. This could take the form of bushwalking or bike-riding or even something a little more adventurous when they get older, such as abseiling or parachuting. They will have a sense of adventure and be afraid of very little.

your Sagittarius child from 7 to 10 years

Responsibility is not something that comes easily to your Sagittarius child. They are too interested in everything else to spend time focusing on what needs to be done. They have been born with an innate need to understand the how and why of all things and people, not with taking care of the necessities of life.

It is important that you introduce your child to the concept of being responsible at this stage, but do not expect them to grasp it quickly. You will need patience and it is important that you persevere. As your child values their freedom so much, you can use this as a bargaining tool. They can go out to play when they have completed the simple chores you set for them. Try to keep tasks simple initially; things they can complete relatively quickly. Once they grasp the concept of reward for action they will be keen to gain more privileges. Your child's motivation comes primarily from inside and it is a matter of tapping into that for success.

> As Sagittarius children come under the influence of the planet Mars, the cell salt that is most of use to them in times of stress is Kali Phos (potassium phosphate). This helps to rebalance the system and can be particularly useful during puberty.

your Sagittarius teen from II to I4 years

As the teenager emerges, it is important that you maintain your lessons in growing responsibility, if you ever want your child to become independent and be able to take care of themself. Your teen is now old enough to be taking care of their own basic needs and should certainly be responsible for simple things such as cleaning their own room and making their bed. Now could also be a good time to teach them how to operate the washing machine and help with the dishes and cooking if they are not already doing so.

Your child is not likely to be overly rebellious at this age but will be challenging, in that they are developing their own belief system and sense of justice. They will question authority and want to know why rules are necessary. Be honest and open in your discussions with your teen. While they may not agree with your opinions, they will respect your authority if it is wielded fairly. If you can maintain the lines of communication through this period and encourage your child to share their views, you will go a long way towards developing a sound adult relationship with them, based on mutual trust and respect.

Your child should now be looking seriously at career options and for them veterinary science, farming, gardening, mechanics and painting are high on the list, statistically speaking. Even though they love to learn and share, they rank quite poorly among teachers and lawyers. Your child needs a career choice that will allow them freedom to move and preferably experience the outdoors as much as possible. An occupation such as park ranger or something similar allows them to combine their passions for working with animals and being outside, perfect for Sagittarians.

The young Sagittarius adult

As your child grows into adulthood they will continue to have a wide range of interests and friends. They are quite sociable and you are likely to catch glimpses of them on rare occasions as they call home for a meal or clean clothes. When they do stay for longer than five minutes, they will want to share with you what they have been doing and they will probably have some interesting tales to tell.

It is important that you continue to encourage their independence by allowing them to be responsible for their own laundry and, if they are in and out, their own meals. Don't fall into the trap of being their free restaurant and laundry. That is having a good time at someone else's expense, not independence. Chances are your child will want to go to college or university and will be at least partially dependent for some time but it needs to be on your terms, not theirs.

Although your Sagittarius child may not stay still long enough to smell the roses, they do enjoy carnations and dandelion flowers and lime, mulberry, ash and birch trees. Perhaps you can plant some together and watch them grow.

Famous Sagittarians

Beethoven

Winston Churchill

Frank Sinatra

Mark Twain

Sammy Davis, Jnr

Walt Disney

Kirk Douglas

Steven Spielberg

Bette Midler

Jane Fonda

Maggie Tabberer

John Flynn

Lew Hoad

Robert Menzies

Robert J. Hawke

Kerry Packer

Ben Stiller

Britney Spears

Teri Hatcher

Brad Pitt

John Larroquette

Georgie Parker

Felicity Huffman

Nelly Furtado

Christina Aguilera

Jamie Foxx

Louisa May Alcott

C.S. Lewis

capricorn child

Ruling Planet—Saturn ♄
Element—Earth
Quality—Cardinal
Sign—the Sea-goat
Glyph—♑
Gemstone—Garnet
Metal—Lead
21 December–20 January

'Childhood is the fiery furnace in which we are melted down to essentials and that essential shaped for good.'

Katherine Anne Porter

Capricorns are noted for having their feet on the ground—some would say firmly stuck in the mud. They are practical, have a good sense of financial matters and an amazing, if somewhat dry, wit and sense of humour. They can have difficulty letting their hair down and may need assistance with learning to relax and have fun, without feeling guilty.

You will often hear people referring to the young Capricorn as an 'old soul'. These babies and children have an aura of wisdom and are said to be born old and grow younger as they age. As children they tend to appear much older than their years and parents sometimes forget how young the child is and expect behaviour or achievements that aren't really age appropriate.

Saturn is the ruling planet affecting Capricorn. How it is placed in the birth horoscope will be the major influence on your child's personality and this explains why all Capricorn children are not the same. For example, the Capricorn child with Saturn in Pisces, Cancer or Scorpio can be more sensitive than the 'average' Capricorn, Saturn in Gemini or Libra can be more scattered, although Aquarius adds mental structure, Saturn in Capricorn, Taurus or Virgo will be more grounded and directed, while Aries, Leo and Sagittarius can provide initiative.

> Saturn is also associated with the day Saturday, and the number eight, so your Capricorn child may find them lucky.

your child's will

From the very beginning your child will respond much better if you speak to them as you would to anybody else. They will not take kindly to baby talk. They will be quite strong-willed and determined and won't make a big fuss in order to get their own way. They will not be into temper tantrums or other obvious displays but will communicate their needs quite effectively.

They will let you know what they want and then patiently wait for your answer. If the answer is no and it wasn't that important they will accept your decision; however, if it was something that they had really set their mind to, they will appear to accept your decision but will keep working at it until they finally get what they were after. This is a child with perseverance and tenacity.

Your child will be solemn, cautious and reserved. They will be strong of mind, ethical and compassionate, often taking the side of the underdog. They will be determined to reach their goals and will begin setting them almost as soon as they are able to. Watch the determination as they try to sit, walk and then reach to the top of the cupboard.

your capricorn baby
from birth to 6 months

- Serious
- Cuddly
- Shy and reserved
- Evokes comments from others about how they must have been here before

- Meets gaze head-on from a very early age
- Intense
- May stiffen or become rigid if they feel threatened or insecure
- Very affectionate and responsive

Enjoys cuddles, being in close contact with parents, feeling secure

Doesn't like feeling helpless

your capricorn baby

When you first gaze into this little one's eyes you may well be intrigued by the seriousness of the gaze that is returned. Capricorn's gaze can be very disconcerting with the wisdom that seems to be held in the eyes of one so young. They appear to understand what is happening around them. The little Capricorn seems to have been born old and often looks like a wrinkled little old man or woman at birth, becoming rounder and more beautiful as the days go by. They will develop into a cuddly and undemanding baby, with a smile that may not be seen often but is worth waiting for.

Your baby will be undemanding as long as their basic needs are met. It is important to cuddle your Capricorn when they are little, as once they begin to grow they will tend to shun this sort of contact. If you give them plenty of affection early on it will be easier for them to show it later. Your child should settle into a routine fairly easily and is generally a steady sleeper and feeder.

your capricorn baby
from 6 to 18 months

- Bright and curious
- Loves to *do* things, particularly imitating adults around them
- Enjoys peek-a-boo and hand and finger games
- Will want to feed themself as soon as they are able
- Will enjoy helping to put away their own toys and clothes
- Loves to spend time outdoors
- Will begin climbing as soon as they are mobile enough to pull themself up on furniture, stairs, etc.
- Needs encouragement to play and explore

Enjoys attention, being taken seriously, reassurance

Doesn't like surprises, being thrown in the air, too much time on their own

your capricorn toddler

As they grow older, they will begin to organise their life into a routine. They will sort their toys in a particular way and particular order and may get upset if someone else disturbs them. They should adapt well to mealtime routine and bath and bedtime schedules and may in fact become a little out of sorts if there is too much deviation.

Even when quite young they will show a preference for home life; they would generally prefer to spend time at home than outside running around with other children. They are unlikely to run around with a large group of friends, preferring a small group of close friends and perhaps just one special friend.

Your child will seem to be always doing something, as they feel the need to be occupied in some useful task all the time. They will enjoy helping adults in the family, gardening, washing the car or even doing housework. Something that will give them both pleasure and a sense of achievement would be their own little garden patch. They will enjoy working with the earth and growing a variety of flowers and vegetables. This could prove a useful way of helping them to relax while still maintaining their need to be busy and useful.

Although they may appear to be a little slower and more methodical than other children, don't be fooled into thinking that they are any less capable. They take a little more time to learn a skill because they want to learn it well. Once they have learnt a skill, they will carry it out with the precision of one way beyond their years.

This is a child who is always a pleasure to take out anywhere; they will always behave themself, be polite and remember their manners. They are sure to inspire comments from your friends and family about what a well-behaved and delightful child they are. They will enjoy adult company and conversation and will be very pleased to be included.

Your child is not spontaneous and will require plenty of notice when required to do something or go somewhere. They enjoy routine and knowing what is going to happen ahead of time. If you are planning an outing for them, they will want to know the plan. If you tell them, 'We are going to visit grandma and do some shopping' and you do it the other way around, they will probably complain that you said you were going to grandma's first.

They are not one to reach out for physical contact, but they love being close and will melt into your arms when you reach out to hug them. Remember, they are reserved, not unloving. If you can encourage them to be a little less reserved and more outgoing when young it will help them to carry these attributes into adulthood.

Your Capricorn child will enjoy working with their hands and creating things for others to use. They will be happiest if all of their things are kept neat and orderly. They will be reliable, practical, determined, capable and thorough. They may also be lacking in self-confidence, which can prevent them from expressing their true potential, so encourage them when young with appropriate praise.

Easy to live with and get along with, your child will rarely make unreasonable demands upon others. They are not particularly untidy or fussy and will eat just about anything as long as it is well cooked. They will enjoy more exotic tastes and, although quite conservative in other ways, can be quite daring when it comes to food.

Toilet training

Toilet training will be tackled in a serious and determined manner. It is usually accomplished fairly quickly. Your child will be very keen to show how grown-up they are and will respond well to sound reason. Usually the fact that everyone else does it will be enough. The little Capricorn can literally go overnight from nappies to using the toilet as long as they are ready; remember not to push your child beyond where they need to be at their age.

your capricorn toddler
from 18 months to 3 years

- Curious
- Seeks information on people and work, and will begin to develop an interest in history, commencing with their own family
- Observant
- Requires explanations
- Usually obedient but can display occasional rebelliousness
- Capable of rationalising their own behaviour—will always have an excuse for bad behaviour
- By the age of three, will have developed an incredible amount of self-control over their emotions and may need encouragement to express feelings
- Continues to need encouragement to explore and play

Enjoys explanations, reasons, firm rules, forgiveness, kindness, help in expressing emotions

Doesn't like being alone, too much responsibility

your child's emotions

The Moon in a birth chart represents your child's emotions and instinctual responses. It is an excellent clue to how they respond in emotional situations. The Moon rules infancy and early childhood, and is the face of your child that you will see most often during the early years.

Emotions are also associated with the element water, as is the Moon. As the Moon waxes and wanes, we see the effects on the tides. It also affects all living beings. The Moon is instinctive, intuitive and empathetic. The Moon reflects the light from the Sun and is associated with similar attributes for your child. The Moon shows how your child deals with mood changes and emotions, how your child learns to become reflective and stores memories.

Your child will be determined and reliable. Their nature is serious and stable. They will be old beyond their years and much too serious for one so young. Their biggest and hardest lesson in life will be learning to relax: they are such serious little things that this is not something that comes easily to them. Practical above everything else, they will find it difficult to just have fun. You will have to teach them that play is good and useful and everything they do doesn't have to have a reason or outcome.

They will find it difficult to express how they feel and may give the impression that they are cold and uncaring; this isn't so. They are unsure of how to respond in an emotional situation. As a result they are likely to be reserved and uncomfortable when meeting new people. They can be shy and self-conscious.

Like their animal counterpart the goat, Capricorn tends be fairly sure-footed. The knees are the most vulnerable part of the body for your child; if they fall, this is the part most likely injured.

It is important that you encourage your child to express their emotions but don't push them or make them feel guilty.

Show them appreciation when they show affection and they will be more likely to repeat it. Don't force them into shows of affection for others. If they want to give someone a hug or kiss, they will; if not, respect their choice and remember they are not naturally demonstrative.

They will show their love by being responsible and dependable. They will do as they are asked, follow the rules of the house and try to live up to your expectations of them. Security is important to them and they will not take very well to changes in their environment.

Capricorn children resonate to earthy colours such as dark grey, black and dark brown, indicative of their serious nature. Although these are the colours they are most comfortable with, it is a good idea to add some vibrant yellow and green and pastel hues to their room and clothing for contrast and to lift their spirit.

your capricorn preschooler

Playtime can be a problem for some Capricorns, as they find it difficult to relax and have fun. Your little child will need your encouragement to play outside in the fresh air and sunshine and to join in with other children. Their reserve and lack of confidence make it difficult for them. They will enjoy a more structured type of play and will excel at games that have clearly defined rules.

Once they learn to overcome their hesitancy amongst their peer group, don't be surprised to see them become the leader. Other children will recognise that they can be trusted to be responsible and are happy to defer to them.

It could be very easy to forget that your child is still a little child, as by around age three or four they will be so responsible you may begin expecting things from them that are really beyond their age. You will need to keep reminding yourself that they are only three, four or five and not the much older child they appear to be. They will take all the responsibility that is put on them, so remember to ask yourself occasionally whether you are being fair with them or expecting too much.

Your Capricorn child has fairly simple tastes. Their preferred foods are potatoes, barley, beets, malt, spinach, onions and quince and you may find it useful to include small amounts of these in their diet once their palate is mature enough to appreciate them. Your child will appreciate whatever you give them as long as it is cooked well.

Your child may find it difficult to ask for help, and offering them your assistance in a way that will not dent their ego will be very important to their self-esteem. They may see asking for help as a sign of weakness. Although they are very generous with their support of others they can become quite annoyed at themself for showing similar needs. In this way they do appear to be quite self-sufficient and can seem resistant to assistance when it is offered. Learning to receive help as well as give it will be a very important lesson for your child.

When it comes time for starting school, your child should settle in quite well. They will be quite studious and enjoy learning, and they will also cope well with routine and regulations. As a rule, homework shouldn't be a huge issue, as they will generally take care of it before they go out to play.

You can help support your child's feelings of self-reliance and independence by offering them loving touches. A gentle hug as they work away on their latest project, an affectionate kiss as you walk by, or other signs of affection and recognition let them know their value.

As they will have a tendency to feel that they must do things alone, regular loving physical contact from those they love helps provide them with the comfort and reassurance they need.

your capricorn preschooler from 3 to 6 years

- Developing 'adult' skills, may alternate between being bossy, critical, judgmental and small, helpless and frustrated
- Intensity and seriousness become even more prominent
- Increased sense of responsibility may tempt adults to place more than their share of responsibility on them
- Begins really testing the limits and boundaries, both their own and those imposed upon them by others
- May become moody and even angry as they define what are their capabilities and what they can expect from others
- By nature a sweet and gentle being, they may become distressed by their own lack of control during this 'testing' phase

- Occasional depression may be experienced, usually manifesting as lethargy or lack of motivation

Needs information, honesty, help when appropriate, security, to understand the rules, boundaries and limits, to feel useful

Doesn't like lack of assistance, needing to ask for help, feeling abandoned

Fun, friendship and confidence

Even though your child may appear on the outside to be self-reliant and resilient, on the inside they are sensitive, shy and vulnerable. They are physically strong and rarely ill—and when they are, you are unlikely to know about it unless they have a high fever or other symptoms that you can see.

Although quite serious, your child has a delightful and offbeat sense of humour. Dry and witty, they will delight you with their unique slant on the world. Your child learns well but is more likely to shine in subjects that are practical, rather than purely academic.

Your child is not likely to take too many chances in life and this may make them appear timid. They aren't, but they weigh up the possible outcome before they attempt something, and if they feel the risks are too great, they won't attempt it.

When they get older they will enjoy playing board games with the rest of the family—Scrabble, Monopoly and a variety of card games will appeal to them. Encourage them to spend time outside playing with friends as well. They will relate very well to adults and may feel more comfortable in their presence than that of other children. They will also need your encouragement to help them mix with their own peer group.

The goat is the animal most associated with Capricorn and this represents their determination and tenacity in life when striving for their goals. There are two representations of the goat, one being the sure-footed mountain goat but the other is the sea-goat—half fish, half goat. It represents the Capricorn affinity with the ocean, which can be a source of calm and peace for them.

First impressions

The ascendant, or rising sign in your child's horoscope is where heaven meets Earth: the part of the sky that is visible on the horizon, looking directly to the east at the time of birth. Some say this represents the soul's entry into the earthly plane. In a birth chart it represents the physical body of an individual and shows how we meet the world head-on. It is referred to as the mask we wear when we first meet people, the filter through which all of the planets within the birth chart are expressed.

With Capricorn on the ascendant, your little child will be of relatively slight build and height. They will tend to have a rather bony appearance with high cheekbones and a wonderful smile. Your child should be quite good-looking and very photogenic. Height and physique will be average to small and although they may be prone to weight gain later in life, they will be on the slight side for the most part.

Your child will be calm, gentle and a little quiet even amongst family and friends. With outsiders they can be quite reserved and shy, uncomfortable with public displays of affection. They will enjoy lots of cuddles and affection within the home but are not openly demonstrative.

They will be quite ambitious and likely to have decided upon a career path at quite a young age. They have the ability and determination to achieve their goals.

They have a strong need for security and are generally very good with managing money. They will be a hard worker and once they have begun a task will follow through until it is completed, no matter how long it takes.

> Your Capricorn comes across to others as quiet, shy, conservative and a little lacking in confidence, while also reliable, resilient and determined.

your capricorn child from 7 to 10 years

Your Capricorn child was born feeling responsible. They will be very dependable and watch out for everyone else. If the family is meant to be somewhere at a particular time, this is the child who will be watching the clock to make sure you aren't late. They will be a hard worker and self-disciplined and trustworthy. They will make great efforts to live up to their commitments and responsibilities. This focus on responsibility is another thing that makes it difficult for them to play, as they can be so serious and intense that they can actually feel guilty for taking time out to relax.

They will want to ensure they have taken care of all the things that need to be done before they can relax. They will enjoy being occupied in practical and useful ways, such as helping in the garden or with the housework. For your Capricorn child, moving into the stage of their development that focuses on their natural strengths and skills is easy. What your child needs to learn now is to balance their responsible side with the ability to relax, enjoy and have fun.

As Capricorn children come under the earthy influence of the planet Saturn, the cell salt that is most of use to them in times of stress is Calc Phos (calcium phosphate). This helps to rebalance the system and can be particularly useful during puberty.

your capricorn teen from 11 to 14 years

Your child will have strong family ties and wherever possible their family will always come first. This doesn't prevent them from going through a little rebellion as they move into their teen years. They can suddenly rail against the responsibility they have previously enjoyed and are likely to challenge your authority. This can be a difficult time for all, but at the same time if it means your child is to lighten up and gain more balance in their life, then it will be worth it in the long run.

Capricorn is quite career oriented but surprisingly, given their reputation, don't rank that highly among business owners. Of course, one of the world's better-known corporate Capricorns was Howard Hughes.

Where they do have a much higher showing is among politicians, scientists, farmers, gardeners, carpenters and mechanics. Whatever their chosen career, they will need a certain level of autonomy and control.

The young capricorn adult

As your teen matures into the young adult, they do so with a relatively smooth flow. The rebelliousness of the teen years is left behind as your child now focuses on their adult future. Your child may not be particularly interested in ecological or humanitarian issues but could be quite interested in politics and will begin exploring this now. Their mind is acute and shrewd and while not necessarily academic, they work methodically. This combination, along with their excellent powers of concentration, will help them work hard and study to achieve their ambitions.

They will have a very dry sense of humour and be quite witty but can still find it difficult to just relax and have fun. Encourage your young adult to lead a balanced lifestyle and to remember there is a spiritual side to life as well as the practical.

Capricorn is associated with red poppy and pansy flowers and willow, pine, elm, yew and poplar trees. It may be helpful to have some of these or pictures of them in your child's space.

Famous capricorns

Humphrey Bogart
Howard Hughes
Joan of Arc
Richard Nixon
Benjamin Franklin
Helena Rubenstein
Rudyard Kipling
Nostradamus
Conrad Hilton
Ita Buttrose
May Gibbs

Johnny O'Keefe
Orlando Bloom
Jim Carrey
Elvis Presley
Maggie Smith
J.R.R. Tolkein
Jack London
Henry Miller
George Foreman
Joe Frazier
Muhammad Ali

Aquarius child

Ruling Planet—Saturn ♄
Element—Air
Quality—Fixed
Sign—the Water bearer
Glyph—♒
Gemstone—Aquamarine
Metal—Aluminium, uranium
20 January–18 February

'There's nothing that can help you understand your beliefs more than trying to explain them to an inquisitive child.'

Frank A. Clark

Aquarians are inherently curious, social, independent, broad-minded, rebellious and adventurous. These traits will appear in different ways at different stages and while certain traits may be more dominant at various times, they are always present. For example, the fear of restriction and abandonment is one that is apparent from the beginning and while it may be overshadowed by other things it is always present in some form.

Your child may be a little shy and is likely to have a quiet and unassuming nature. As they grow they will become very popular and they are likely to have many friends. They will be affectionate and kind and will enjoy listening to the opinions of others and sharing and exchanging ideas.

Saturn is the ruling planet affecting Aquarius. How it is placed in the birth horoscope will be the major influence on your child's personality and this explains why all Aquarius children are not the same. For example, the Aquarius child with Saturn in Pisces, Cancer or Scorpio can be more sensitive than the 'average' Aquarius, Saturn in Gemini or Libra can be more outgoing, Saturn in Capricorn, Taurus or Virgo will be more grounded and directed, while Aries, Leo and Sagittarius can provide initiative.

> Saturn is also associated with the day Saturday, and the number eight, so your Aquarius child may find them lucky.

your child's will

Aquarius is one of the intellectual or thinking signs and children born under this sign usually have a deep and inquiring mind with strong intuition. They are likely to enjoy science, literature and philosophy when they get older.

They will be incredibly persistent in whatever they undertake and, as a result of this, they are likely to succeed in the long run with whatever path they choose. They take great pride in their friends and loved ones and delight in the success of others.

Your child will be strong-willed and very definite in their likes and dislikes. They will be willing to do anything for those they care for but will resent any attempts to force them in a certain direction. In fact, under these circumstances they may become extremely stubborn. They will be generally quite set in their opinions and attitudes and once an opinion has been formed they will not change it easily.

your Aquarius baby from birth to 6 months

- Bright and lively
- Alert and responds well to people and objects
- Short attention span, easily distracted
- Loves surprise
- Enjoys gentle physical games
- Doesn't like physical restriction, including clothing or bedding
- Likes being talked to and interacting with others
- Enjoys sensory stimulation

Needs time alone, with the reassurance that there is someone near

Doesn't like restriction, abandonment

your Aquarius baby

One of the first things you'll notice with your baby Aquarian is their curiosity, sparkling eyes and a strong sense of their own identity. Your baby will be alert and spend their waking time taking in the world around them. They may take time to settle into a regular routine and can be light sleepers. They will not respond so well to being tightly wrapped and will enjoy having part of the day to kick the air with their nappy off.

As a young baby and small child they will have a fear of abandonment but nevertheless enjoy time alone. This in turn will become one of the greatest dilemmas for you as a parent, in trying to judge how much freedom and independence to give your child. They will enjoy gentle physical games and contact but may become uncomfortable, tense and even irritable with too much physical contact and any form of physical restriction or confinement. They will tend to lie in their crib when they wake, quietly chatting to themself until you come in to check on them, unless they are in desperate need of a nappy change or feed.

your Aquarius baby from 6 to 18 months

- Becoming increasingly interested in surroundings
- Curious and restless
- Has little sense of danger and needs to be watched (from a distance) to avoid accidents and mishaps resulting from their curiosity
- May walk and talk early

- Rebellion sets in between twelve to eighteen months; will continually test the boundaries

Needs open space, stimulation, supervision, reassurance and quiet time

Doesn't like restriction, abandonment

your Aquarius toddler

Despite what is written in many of the popular astrology magazines, Aquarians are very sensitive. They are easily hurt and can take a long time to heal.

You will find it rather difficult to keep your toddler covered, as they will not enjoy being tightly tucked in and will tend to kick their blankets off as soon as they are able. They may be quite a restless sleeper and may wake themself up often during the night as they toss and turn. Your child is also likely to be a light sleeper and it would be mutually beneficial to get them used to sleeping with sound and activity going on around them. You could do this by having a radio playing in their room when they sleep and by going about your normal activities rather than trying to keep the house totally quiet.

Your child will be alert and quick to respond to people or objects in their immediate vicinity but likely to have a short attention span when they are very young. They will generally respond well to the element of surprise or the unexpected, so things like a game of peek-a-boo will have them enchanted. They will also respond well to anything bright or sparkly and you may find that they respond much better to strong, bright colours than to soft pastels.

As they get older, your child is more likely to enjoy parallel activities; where two or more people are in close proximity but engaged in independent tasks or activities. So they may enjoy sitting on the kitchen floor playing with their toys while you prepare a meal. This gives them reassurance and closeness and their need for freedom and independence.

Your toddler requires gentle encouragement and clear and concise instructions. They will enjoy toys and games that test their logic and thinking ability, such as stacking cups or shape-sorters when very little, and puzzles as they grow. This is a good time to introduce your child to the computer, VCR and so on as their natural curiosity will lead that way anyway— teach your child the correct way to use these tools and there should be no major mishaps.

An aspect that you, as parent, may find frustrating is the feeling of detachment you may feel at times from your child. This may lead to you not being sure how to approach them or to reach them. They may appear sometimes flighty or spaced out, while at other times they don't seem to hear you at all. You may ask them several times to do something and half an hour later they are still sitting in the same place. Their mind can become so engrossed in whatever they are thinking about at the time that they just don't hear you.

Verbal communication is the best way to connect with your Aquarius child and to help them learn to focus attention. They will enjoy communicating with you, talking about what they are doing and what you are doing. They love to talk and listen and when older will want their opinions heard as well. They will want to understand how everything fits together, from the parts in the VCR to where they fit in the family, social circle and the world in general.

Your child will be independent, talkative, thoughtful and cooperative, while at the same time needing space and respect for their freedom and individuality. They will enjoy company of both their peers and adults but they will challenge you if they feel you are being unfair.

They will be delightful and engaging and need to know that they are loved even though they enjoy physical contact in moderation. They will not respond well to being confined and restricted. They will delight and puzzle you with a well-developed but very dry sense of humour.

Toilet training

Toilet training your Aquarius child can be a difficult time. Try to take a logical approach rather than an emotive one. The child will feel uncomfortable with undue attention being paid to their physical body and will not respond well to any form of physical or emotional pressure. A simple explanation of what is required is the best approach, and then let your child respond in their own time. You may well be amazed at how quickly they 'train' themself.

your Aquarius toddler from 18 months to 3 years

- Curiosity increases
- Analytical mind kicks in; needs to know and understand how everything fits together
- Puzzles would be a good plaything during this stage
- Becoming more social and will enjoy interacting with peers

- Logic is developing; may become argumentative
- Behaviour can become unpredictable

Needs brief but clear explanations, few but firm limits, a wide variety of experiences, the ability to explore safely and to be allowed to become more independent

Doesn't like too much independence, lack of boundaries, being ignored

your child's emotions

The Moon in a birth chart represents your child's emotions and instinctual responses. It is an excellent clue to how they respond in emotional situations. The Moon rules infancy and early childhood, and is the face of your child that you will see most often during the early years.

Emotions are also associated with the element water, as is the Moon. As the Moon waxes and wanes, we see the effects on the tides. It also affects all living beings. The Moon is instinctive, intuitive and empathetic. The Moon reflects the light from the Sun and is associated with similar attributes for your child. The Moon shows how your child deals with mood changes and emotions, how your child learns to become reflective and stores memories.

Your Aquarius Moon child will be emotionally independent and may even seem cool and distant at times. There will be a tendency to keep their feelings bottled up and although at times they may be emotionally reserved, they still need you to show them how much they are loved.

When they meet someone for the first time your child may be a little shy; watch them though, as they quietly take the measure of this new acquaintance. They will generally be kind and helpful towards others, with a humanitarian leaning. They are more than happy to be helpful in practical ways but could feel at a total loss when faced with an emotional situation.

Aquarius does not have an animal symbol. Its image is a man pouring water. This symbolises the waters of life and their desire for humanity, hence the connection of Aquarius with 'causes'. In their searching for answers, they can spend too much time with their head in the clouds and this leaves them susceptible to minor accidents, with the ankles as the most vulnerable part of the body.

Your child is likely to have an excellent and quick mind, with strong intuition. They will also be inventive and able to come up with wonderful ideas, with the ability to put them into practice. They will develop a rather dry sense of humour as they grow, and this reflects their rather offbeat inner nature. Your child would prefer to follow their own direction than be just one of the crowd. They will enjoy learning and expanding their mind; don't be surprised to find them expanding yours at the same time.

They will be for the most part sensible but prepared to accept most of life's challenges. People will warm to their friendliness and they will be friendly in return. Your child will not discriminate against anyone because of their colour, race, religion or age. They don't see any of these things when they weigh up an individual. They will have high standards in both honesty and integrity and no interest in petty issues.

Aquarius children resonate to the colours aquamarine, turquoise and electric blue. They will feel very comfortable wearing these colours and using them in their surroundings. It would be advisable to use them in the colour scheme of their room to promote physical and emotional wellbeing.

your Aquarius preschooler

You need to be very clear about the rules for your preschooler. They will continually test the boundaries but need to know boundaries are there in order to feel secure. You need to set firm limits but not too many. Be realistic as to what you are, and aren't, willing to accept. Be firm once you have set the rules, for if your little Aquarian sees the slightest chink in the armour they will continually push at it until you give in.

As your child grows, so will their desire to mix with others their own age and, later, those who share their interests. They will enjoy playgroup or preschool, as this gives them the opportunity to be social. If your child becomes withdrawn at this stage and keeps too much to their own company there is generally a reason and it needs to be discovered and dealt with before it becomes a bigger problem. They will do best in an environment that allows freedom within structure. They want to conform and be just like the rest of the kids but at the same time they need to be free to express their own personality.

They may express themself by painting a picture of a house like all of the other children but theirs will be painted using all purple instead of the multitude of colours that the other children have used. As they get older, they may wear the school uniform but add something of themself to it, perhaps coloured shoelaces or a slightly different colour to some part of the uniform. This represents both their need and desire to conform, while at the same time expressing their difference.

The Aquarian foods are apples, citrus fruits and all dried fruits. You may find it useful to include small amounts of these in their diet once their palate is mature enough to appreciate them.

They are quick to grasp new concepts and should have no trouble adjusting to school when the time comes, although they may prefer to skip kindergarten and move straight up with the 'big kids' who are doing 'real work'. Your child will challenge teachers if they believe they are incorrect in either premise or practice and will readily jump to the defence of anyone they feel is being persecuted. They will begin honing their skills as defender of the underdog from a very young age.

Your child will be drawn to anyone or anything that is unusual and a little outside the norm. They will be very accepting and tolerant of the differences in people and will not be prone to judging on any grounds. They will challenge many accepted ways of categorising people and find the whole concept of divisions based on creed, colour, nationality and so on difficult to understand, seeing everyone as individuals. They can become involved in 'causes' from a young age as they will see inequality and want to play their part in correcting the balance.

Your Aquarius child needs to feel that they are recognised for themself. They need praise and recognition and if this doesn't come for the positive things they do, they may begin to seek it by misbehaving or doing extraordinary things. The one thing they will not be able to tolerate is indifference or being ignored. Your child will seek your attention one way or another.

The form that recognition takes is also important: quiet displays of praise are best. They may feel that they risk being alienated from their friends or peers if undue attention is paid to them. They need to know they are valued without it compromising their position in the group. This is a dilemma faced by all Aquarians and those within their intimate circle. They need to stand out from the crowd while at the same time blending in. It is a balancing act that will take quite a while to achieve. Parents can help by teaching them to take pleasure in their achievements without the accompanying guilt. Let them know that pride in one's own achievements and accomplishments is not a bad thing.

your Aquarius preschooler from 3 to 6 years

- Will revel in preschool as they become more socially orientated
- Is increasingly curious and may become restless and unruly unless there is enough mental stimulation
- Reason and logic are really starting to develop now; will argue and debate with anyone and everyone
- May become detached if restricted too much or embarrassed in any way

- Needs time on their own but also needs the company of others who share their interests

Needs to mix with the peer group, brief explanations, choices and options, quiet time, understanding, few but firm boundaries

Doesn't like restriction or confinement, being excluded or isolated

fun, friendship and confidence

Your Aquarian will be generally easygoing and kind. While they may cope with disruption and chaos outside the home, when they are at home they prefer peace. They like to be in control of their surroundings, and this is one of the things they need for their own emotional wellbeing.

They will be attracted to the unique and unusual. They will learn and understand concepts quite easily and enjoy science, maths and electronics. They may also want to investigate subjects such as astrology.

Your little Aquarian will enjoy company but may not take it too kindly if they feel they have no choice in the situation. For example, if you have a friend who calls in fairly regularly and brings a child, you may expect your child to let them into their room and play with their toys. The problem is your Aquarius child may not even like this other child and even if they did, they would resent the expectations you have placed on them. This doesn't mean that they are either selfish or mean-spirited; they just like to have a choice.

When they get a little older they will enjoy mixing in groups, perhaps beginning with playgroup and gradually building to organisations such as cubs, scouts or something similar, eventually leading to a mix of social and charitable pursuits, such as a service club, when they reach adulthood.

Your child may have a bit of a temper problem when they are quite young but with your help they will learn to control it.

Your child won't like loud or discordant noises and will need their own space, preferably with a large yard to run around in. If you don't have access to a large yard, try to take them to a park or other large open space as often as possible. They need a certain amount of freedom in choosing their own play activities and will need to be outdoors for part of the day. This is a child who will not like being cooped up or fenced in. They will enjoy exploring new places and discovering new things to play with or do. They will want to choose their own clothes from a young age and their taste may differ dramatically from what you would choose for them. They will develop their own unique style in everything they do, from clothing, to learning, to the foods they prefer.

Although Aquarius is one of the human signs, there are a number of animals associated with the sign. Among them are the wolf, elephant and peacock. These all represent different facets of the Aquarian personality: loyal, immovable and just a little arrogant.

First impressions

The ascendant, or rising sign in your child's horoscope is where heaven meets Earth: the part of the sky that is visible on the horizon, looking directly to the east at the time of birth. Some say this represents the soul's entry into the earthly plane. In a birth chart it represents the physical body of an individual and shows how we meet the world head-on. It is referred to as the mask we wear when we first meet people, the filter through which all of the planets within the birth chart are expressed.

With Aquarius on the rise, your child will have a mind of their own. They will be smallish in stature compared to other family members, and quite compact. They will have the most amazing bright eyes and their smile will light up any room.

You will find them a quite delightful and entertaining child and they will be quite self-sufficient from an early age and able to amuse themself. Your child will tend to be outgoing as they grow and very chatty and friendly to everyone. They will find it easy to make friends and will have many of all ages and shapes and sizes, and your child will.

They will be very determined and you may find it difficult if you are drawn into a battle of wills with them. They can be reasoned with, however, and if you appeal to their sense of fair play they will respond. Your child is not into emotional blackmail or emotional games of any kind; you need to be straight with them if you want their cooperation.

Your child operates more on the intellectual level than the emotional when dealing with others and uses logic to weigh up a situation. Offer them logic and they will be far more likely to see your perspective or point of view than if you try to get to them through tears or hysterics.

your Aquarius child from 7 to 10 years

With the development of responsibility there should be minimum conflict with your Aquarius child. The Aquarian energy is one of cooperation and equality, so you will find that your child will cooperate beautifully, as long as they agree with what you are asking of them. Remember, they need to see the logic. They are likely to find themself in leadership positions because of their sense of fair play.

Your child needs to be given responsibility in small manageable doses, with clear instructions. They will carry out their tasks without too much fuss but will let you know if they feel they are doing more than their fair share. Your child needs firm guidelines at this stage and even though they may complain, it is important they understand that rules are there for a reason. It is also important that the rules are fair and apply equally to everyone, otherwise that is where your child will rebel.

As Aquarius children come under the influence of the air rulership of the planet Saturn, the cell salt that is of most use to them in times of stress is Nat Mur (sodium chloride). This helps rebalance the system and can be particularly useful during puberty.

your Aquarius teen from 11 to 14 years

Although Aquarius is the sign of the rebel, your Aquarian will not be any more rebellious than the average teen. They will want to do their thing as always, but can show remarkable maturity when placed in a position of responsibility. Your child is quite often able to perceptively assess situations in a way that is often beyond the vision of those much older and supposedly more knowledgeable.

They will look to you for more freedom and with this comes trust. This will be their argument: if you don't allow them to go somewhere or do something, it is because you don't trust them. You still need to keep firm rules and boundaries in place but now this is best done in discussion with your child. Agree on the rules and the punishment for breaking them. Allow your child to participate in a democratic decision-making process that they can't then complain about later.

Career choices are quite diverse for your Aquarius child and it is no surprise that Aquarius ranks way up on the scale for self-employment. They also tip the scales in farming, physiotherapy and teaching. Your child may also be drawn to professions such as psychology and architecture but will not be so keen on an executive position, bookkeeping, computing or banking. Your Aquarian will be happier where they have some level of self-determination and are not cooped up in a small office from nine to five.

The young Aquarius adult

As the adult emerges you will find your Aquarian offspring is now developing quite an interest in politics and you may be in for some interesting discussions. They will be developing quite strong views and they will usually be coloured by what they see is wrong in the world. This is the person who has all the answers and knows how to fix it.

They can be quite belligerent when it comes to their views and if you want them to develop an open mind, then you need to do so as well. Hear them out, debate with them, even argue but don't shout them down or fob them off. They will look at different systems and may embrace other philosophies but they need to explore and discover in order to find their truth.

Aquarius has an affinity with flowers such as the orchid, apple blossom, lemon blossom and peach blossom, as well as cherry, pear and plum trees. Having these plants, or pictures of them, around your home can work well for your child.

Famous Aquarians

Charles Darwin

James Dean

Abraham Lincoln

George Burns

Lewis Carroll

Thomas Edison

Charles Kingsford Smith

Mia Farrow

Greg Norman

Andrew 'Banjo' Paterson

Oprah Winfrey

Paul Newman

Jennifer Aniston

Ian 'Molly' Meldrum

Ellen DeGeneres

James Spader

Paris Hilton

Natalie Imbruglia

Brandy

Shakira

Justin Timberlake

Alicia Keys

John Travolta

Robbie Williams

John 'Rove' McManus

Wolfgang Amadeus Mozart

Charles Dickens

Mario Lanza

Anton Chekhov

Franz Schubert

Pisces child

Ruling Planet—Jupiter ♃
Element—Water
Quality—Mutable
Sign—the Fishes
Glyph—)(
Gemstone—Amethyst, bloodstone
Metal—Platinum, tin
19 February–20 March

'Some men see things as they are and say, "Why?"
I dream of things that never were and say, "Why not?"'

George Bernard Shaw

Pisces are sweet, soft, cuddly and vulnerable. They can appear more fragile than they really are and parents sometimes need to remind themselves that their Pisces child is not a porcelain doll. They need protection, love and cuddles but also freedom to explore. They are very sensitive to the moods and emotions, as well as the expectations of others, with strong intuition.

Your child will be very creative and can show a talent in music, art or dance. They are likely to be quite shy when young, until their confidence builds. They are trusted and faithful friends and will put the welfare of others before their own.

Jupiter is the ruling planet affecting Pisces. How it is placed in the birth horoscope will be the major influence on your child's personality and this explains why all Pisces children are not the same. The Pisces child with Jupiter in Pisces will express the sensitive, creative side of Pisces, whereas Aries, Leo and Sagittarians can be adventurous, even reckless, Jupiter in Gemini will tend to be more openly communicative, while Jupiter in Capricorn, Taurus or Virgo will be more grounded and directed. The child with a Scorpio Jupiter can be serious, while in Gemini, Libra or Aquarius more curious.

Jupiter is also associated with the day Thursday, and the number seven, so your Pisces child may find them lucky.

your child's will

Although this dreamy child may appear to be malleable, don't be fooled into thinking that you can shape them whichever way you wish. They will get their own way just as surely as the screaming, red-faced Aries child, the commanding Leo child or the stubborn little Taurean. They will get their way by charming you with their sweet smile and magical ways.

Your Pisces lives the life of Peter Pan or Alice in Wonderland, and no matter how old, they retain a childish, dreamy, magical quality of make-believe. Your child will know all about the world of the fairy and will revel when you join them in their make-believe world. They will have the ability to bring out the 'inner child' in even the most hardened adult. It is almost impossible not to join them in their make-believe, at least for short periods.

They can have a tendency to be timid or a little shy when confronted with new people or situations. They prefer to sit back quietly observing until they become comfortable. Don't be surprised if they become particularly clingy at around six to eighteen months. You may find you cannot leave the room without them going into hysterics.

your Pisces baby
from birth to 6 months

- Vulnerable
- Charming
- Adaptable
- Snuggly
- Enjoys the company of others but withdraws periodically into their own little dream world
- Sensitive, and will respond to the moods and emotions around them

- Frightens and startles easily and needs gentle handling
- Enjoys music and being rocked

Needs attention and plenty of physical and verbal affection

Doesn't like feeling insecure, especially the feeling of falling (don't throw this baby in the air)

your Pisces baby

We are all familiar with the myths of babies being found in cabbage patches, or brought from on high by the stork. The new little Pisces baby, however, seems to come special delivery from a mystical fantasy land, complete with moonbeams clutched tightly in their chubby little fists and stardust in their eyes.

Your baby will be relatively placid and easygoing. This is a baby who will generally sleep quite well and has no major problems where feeding is concerned, although they can be a little colicky. Bathtime will be a source of pleasure for you both as your baby will find this a very soothing and calming time and so should you. Massage is also useful for settling your young Pisces should they become fractious. Very gentle massage with some lavender or chamomile oils blended in a light carrier oil is perfect.

your Pisces baby from 6 to 18 months

- Fears strangers and will withdraw if approached
- Benefits from early lessons in swimming, as this child will have a fascination for water

- Enjoys music, both as a listener and making their own
- Creativity and imagination are obvious
- Sensitive and compassionate
- Becoming ever more aware of the emotional climate
- Will begin adapting behaviour to 'fit' others

Needs to be encouraged to express feelings, affection, constant and consistent caring touch

Doesn't like feeling alone

your Pisces toddler

When you gaze into the deep reflective pools that are your child's eyes, what you see reflected back is the magic that they bring with them. The Pisces child does have a somewhat enchanted aura about them and will drift in and out of dreams and fantasy all of their life.

Forget about routines where your toddler is concerned; they will follow their own beat and not that of a ticking clock. They may prefer to sleep all day, have their dinner at midnight and greet the dawn in play. There is something magical about watching the sunrise with a special little person curled up on your lap, reading their favourite fairy story. Of course you may not see it this way if you have a train to catch and need to be fresh for work. The thing is, this is not a routine child and while you may need to eventually get them into a routine, it will be a slow process.

The toddler stage can be a particularly trying time for you all, as you may not even be able to go to the bathroom without them banging on the door and crying from the other side.

Try to be patient with them during this time as they are slowly learning to separate their own identity from yours. As frustrating as this can be for you, it is just as frightening for them, as they realise just how big the world outside is and how tiny they are.

This can be a very important time for building your child's confidence and allowing them to eventually face the world head-on. If they learn during this period that they can venture out slowly but there is always a pair of warm, reassuring arms to run back to, it can help to give them the confidence they will need when the time comes for them to step out on their own.

The sign of Pisces is associated with the feet and there is generally something unusual about the Pisces foot. It can be small in proportion to the rest of the body, or so big that you wonder if they will ever grow into their feet. The Pisces child is a delight to watch when they first master the art of crawling and then walking. The feet resemble the little flippers on a turtle or baby seal as they glide along the floor. Once established on their feet they seem to float or glide along rather than walk. Although generally light on their feet they do have a problem with tripping over objects and regularly stubbing toes.

Your child will enjoy all of the cuddles and physical contact you can give them. They are likely to be somewhat of a 'clingy' baby and will need to know where you are. They will follow you from one end of the house to the other, as soon as they are able and if you aren't carrying them, they are likely to be hanging off your leg. Don't worry too much about spoiling them by carrying and cuddling, as this is what they need in order to feel emotionally secure. The more of this you give them when they are young, the more they are likely to become confident and independent as they grow.

Your child will be strongly intuitive and sensitive. They are able to read the feelings and emotions of those around them. They can become upset sometimes and it is difficult to understand why. Quite often in these circumstances, they're expressing the feelings of somebody around them. So, if you are upset or angry don't be surprised to see those same emotions reflected in your little child.

They will have a wonderful imagination and be capable of creating their own fantasy world. Don't be surprised if when they begin to speak they announce that they have a friend that no one else can see. Your child is likely to have an 'imaginary' playmate who may tell them to do things that they would normally lack the confidence or daring to try. Imaginary friends can be quite a positive influence as this fantasy can provide an outlet that allows them to explore and express different parts of their personality. Do not ridicule your child or dismiss their fantasy. You don't have to encourage them if that is your choice; on the other hand, this can be quite beneficial to boosting their confidence.

Your child will have a natural affinity with water and it is a good idea to take them to swimming lessons as early as possible. They will find the water soothing and relaxing and will generally enjoy their bathtime. You will also find that they are drawn to large bodies of water, hence the need for swimming lessons. They will be fascinated by the way the Sun twinkles and plays on the surface and although they are developing fear they have no real sense of danger. I know my sister was glad of my suggestion of early swimming lessons when her Pisces toddler fell into a backyard swimming pool while leaning over to look into the depths.

Toilet training

Toilet training can be a difficult time for a little Piscean. Your child can learn to use the toilet quite well initially but has difficulty in maintaining this achievement. This child is preoccupied and has difficulty in staying focused on the task at hand. More often than not they will just forget. Rewards and lots of praise for success are the best approach. Do not use harsh punishment or any form of verbal bullying and especially do not belittle or cause them to feel ashamed. Expect that they will take a little longer to get the hang of this and allow them to achieve it in their own time with no pressure. When they are ready it will all fall into place, although you can still expect occasional accidents, particularly during the night. Remember to stay calm and patient and don't make a big issue of it.

your Pisces toddler from 18 months to 3 years

- Intuition is developing, along with the imagination and fantasy
- Likely to have an 'imaginary' playmate
- Music and art becoming more important
- Creativity can really begin to blossom if encouraged
- Can be messy and unpredictable

- Needs sensible limits and boundaries, accurate and clear information

Needs an outlet for their imagination and fantasy while at the same time receiving reminders about reality

Doesn't like to be ignored or feeling invisible, being bored or limited or feeling insecure or unsafe

your child's emotions

The Moon in a birth chart represents your child's emotions and instinctual responses. It is an excellent clue to how they respond in emotional situations. The Moon rules infancy and early childhood, and is the face of your child that you will see most often during the early years.

Emotions are also association with the element water, as is the Moon. As the Moon waxes and wanes, we see the effects on the tide. It also affects all living beings. The Moon is instinctive, intuitive and empathetic. The Moon reflects the light from the Sun and is associated with similar attributes for your child. The Moon shows how your child deals with mood change and emotions, how your child learns to become reflective and stores memories.

Your Pisces Moon child is a very sensitive and gentle little soul. They will have a somewhat dreamy nature and will be very sensitive to the needs and feelings of those around them. They will be on the optimistic side but may tend to look at the world, and those in it, through 'rose-coloured glasses'. They will be very forgiving, as they prefer to see the good in people and believe everyone deserves a second chance. They need to be shown, from a young age, not to let others take advantage of their good nature.

> The feet are the most vulnerable part of the body for your Pisces child, and they will have a tendency to fall over their own feet regularly.

They will be shy in group situations at first and slow to move too far away from you. Gently encourage them in this area, as pushing them too far, too soon, will only make them less willing to separate from you in the future. They need to feel secure before they will be willing to move too far afield.

Your child can be a picky eater and will probably prefer fish, chicken and fruit and vegetables to a lot of red meat. They are also likely to wean themself off milk quite early with a preference for fruit juice. This can lead to problems with their teeth later, so make sure they get their calcium in some other form—cheese, yoghurt, or a supplement. Their appetite will improve as they get older but you may think at times they seem to starve themself; don't worry, they won't. Provide them with lots of small nutritious snacks until they develop a normal eating pattern, which may not happen until they start school.

> Pisces children resonate to the colours sea green, silver, mauve, purple and violet. It is a good idea to use these colours in their room and in their clothing to promote a healthy body and spirit. A touch of more vibrant yellow, orange or red can be used to boost their confidence and energy levels.

your Pisces preschooler

One of the most elusive signs of the Zodiac, Pisces is a water sign, and along with its symbol the fish is associated with the ocean, great depths and changeable surface. Within this sign are the widest range and least predictable patterns of behaviour. Your child can be intensely sensitive and respond to the expectations of others, often to the detriment of their own wellbeing. They may adopt a variety of roles and behaviours that can reflect parental expectations, rather than asserting their own personality.

Your child is adept at picking up messages, particularly those that are unspoken. Their behaviour can often reflect the underlying expectations within the family. They can mirror the collective consciousness of the family and this mirror can reflect both positive and negative images. Your Pisces child can and will act as an emotional barometer for the rest of the family. When all is well in the family they will be happy and outgoing; when there is tension or upset they are likely to respond by withdrawing or with 'out of character' outbursts of anger. You have a very intuitive child and there is no point in trying to hide the truth from them.

Cucumber, rockmelon, watermelon, lettuce and other 'watery' vegetables and fruits plus fish will be the preferred menu for your Pisces child.

Your child may prefer the company of adults to playing with other children, as from a very young age they possess wisdom and understanding way beyond their years. Their sense of reality may differ greatly from yours, and they may be accused of telling lies when they are indeed telling their version of the truth. They have such a vivid imagination and rich fantasy life that they may have difficulty at times in distinguishing reality from fantasy. Your child is so sensitive that they will retreat often into their imagination, which helps them to cope with reality.

Teachers may have difficulty in knowing just what to do with your child when they start school, as they will fit neither into a round nor a square hole. They will be creative and artistic and enjoy music and dancing. Their mind is creative and does not work in a linear fashion. They learn best when combining several of their senses at the one time so find it easiest to learn by doing, rather than watching or listening. The Pisces child is quite often mistaken in a school situation as a 'slow learner', when in fact they simply learn things in a different way. Don't ever underestimate the intellectual capabilities of this child.

They will need constant reassurance in this area, as they will doubt their own abilities. They see that they learn differently and that they perceive things differently to the other children in their class. Their natural tendency is to think that this is because they are not as smart. Encourage them as much as possible to express their own natural talents, allow them access to paints and paper and music. As they may have difficulty in expressing themself verbally, teaching them self-expression through painting, drawing, music or writing either poetry or stories helps them to release their emotions in a positive and creative fashion. This is also an excellent way of harnessing their imagination and natural talents. It can also assist them to separate fantasy and reality.

Your child needs your assistance developing patience and an understanding of consequences for actions.

your Pisces preschooler from 3 to 6 years

- Dreamy and rebellious
- Can be erratic and experience major mood/personality swings
- Still seeking comfort in fantasy and may continually challenge 'reality'
- Curious, bright and very much in tune with the world around them
- Literal in understanding of information and has trouble understanding abstract thoughts
- Can be fascinated with the subjects of God and death
- Empathetic and compassionate and can be easily upset by cruelty or injustice
- Parents should watch closely for feelings of guilt or responsibility for events that do not belong with the child

Needs reassurance, creativity, to be believed

Doesn't like ridicule, being rushed

Fun, friendship and confidence

Your child is sensitive, dreamy, artistic, empathetic, extremely loving and looks at the world through rose-coloured glasses. Treat them gently, with compassion and sensitivity and like an exotic flower they will grow into the most amazing bloom. Allow them to be creative and imaginative, encourage their natural talents and abilities. Give them all the love and support that they need and they in turn will grow into a strong, self-assured young adult.

They will enjoy spending time exploring their musical and artistic talents. They will also enjoy water play and find the feel of water calming. They will want to learn to swim when quite young and find any form of water sport a pleasure.

Your child will prefer being indoors, and creative activities to rowdy outdoor games but will enjoy going for long walks. Expect a steady flow of injured animals, birds and even insects to come through your home: you have here a budding Dr Dolittle. They will always take the side of the underdog and will not tolerate injustice if they can help in any way.

They will enjoy just spending time with those they love and are as content to curl up on a comfy chair while you read them a book as they are with taking walks in the park. They will not be a naturally athletic child and will need your encouragement to play actively outside. They will enjoy dance of any form.

Pisces has an affinity with seals and dolphins. They represent the fluidity of the Pisces nature, their affinity to water and their strong intuition.

First impressions

The ascendant, or rising sign in your child's horoscope is where heaven meets Earth: the part of the sky that is visible on the horizon, looking directly to the east at the time of birth. Some say this represents the soul's entry into the earthly plane. In a birth chart it represents the physical body of an individual and shows how we meet the world head-on. It is referred to as the mask we wear when we first meet people, the filter through which all of the planets within the birth chart are expressed.

Pisces on the ascendant gives a slim body as a young child, with a tendency to a more corpulent or fleshy appearance with a well-rounded body when older. Of average height, your child will have a paler complexion and hair than the overall family colouring. The eyes will be distinctive, large and lustrous.

Your child comes across as quite a shy and reserved individual when first meeting people. It takes them a while to relax and feel comfortable in an unfamiliar situation. They are friendly but need time to sum up a situation or person before they show their true identity.

They will be quite creative and artistic and this can be a good way to help them express themself. Expose them to art and music as early as possible and allow them to use these mediums to overcome their lack of confidence, where possible. It is amazing how a child who has difficulty in saying what they feel can be extremely expressive through art, music or creative writing. It is an excellent way for them to expend their energy and an ideal outlet for frustration.

Your child will be a little on the shy side and may lack a little in self-confidence. You can help them best in this area by encouraging them to try new things and meet new people. Do it slowly and gently though; do not force them in a situation where they feel uncomfortable.

your Pisces child from 7 to 10 years

At this stage in your child's development, it is now time to learn about responsibility. This can be a difficult concept for your Pisces child because as they grow they may show a complete lack of responsibility. They can be quite casual in regard to set tasks and will tend to do the bare minimum—just enough to keep everyone satisfied. Your child tends to be restless, and though they mean to be serious in their approach, they are easily distracted. They need to be able to take frequent breaks when working for extended periods. When setting your child small chores, keep this in mind and break larger tasks into several smaller steps. Praise them when they successfully complete something and encourage them to keep trying when unsuccessful. This can be an important stage in the development of your child's confidence, so you don't want to set them up for defeat.

Your child can be unrealistic about time management and may need help in setting goals and allocating appropriate time for completing tasks. Even when it appears that they are procrastinating, they are probably off in some fantasy world, fighting dragons or solving the problem of the world food shortage. The little Pisces is rarely idle, despite appearances to the contrary. What they need to do now is to harness and direct their energy into the practical world.

As Pisces children come under the influence of the planet Jupiter, the cell salt that is most of use to them in times of stress is Ferr Phos (iron phosphate). This helps rebalance the system and can be particularly useful during puberty.

your Pisces teen
from 11 to 14 years

Your Pisces teen will probably drift through this stage with little change to their usual approach to life. They are highly unlikely to become a rebellious teenager but can be easily led down paths you would prefer they didn't go. I am very much against parents choosing their children's friends but with the Pisces child it is an idea to be a little more vigilant as to their choices. Expose them to safe environments where they are less likely to become involved with those who may lead them into temptation. You can't lock your child in a tower, and ultimately they will go their own way, but if you provide them with options it lessens the chance that they will go the 'wrong' way.

You need firm boundaries in place such as curfews, places that are out of bounds, and homework that needs to be done before playing, watching TV, and so on. Your child will generally follow instructions, as well as they are able. They may not be very good with keeping to time; buying them a watch may be of benefit, but you should still expect that they will lose track of time occasionally.

When it comes to career choices your Pisces child may not have any idea as to what they want to do. Your child could do well at any number of professions but will not be so keen to be tied to a desk, working with figures or computers, unless as a game designer. Statistically, Pisces rank quite highly among farmers, teachers, mechanics, nurses and psychologists, so one of these careers may appeal to your child. Pisces also rank highly among artists and musicians, particularly composers.

The young Pisces adult

When moving into the adult stage your young Pisces can blossom into quite the little socialite. Your formerly reserved and even shy child becomes one of the 'in crowd' and seems to always have somewhere to go. It is important that the firm boundaries and rules remain in place until your child is legally an adult. This is the only way your child will understand, even if only loosely, what rules are for and how to fit in.

Your now young adult will continue to move forward in life cautiously and it is good for them to have a parent they feel they can confide in without judgment. Having an open line of communication with your child is mutually beneficial, as while they may not confide everything to you, they will, through their discussions, give you enough information about where their head is at. This will also be useful for them when discussing their options for their future and to help them sort through their choices. They can become confused as to which direction to take, and being able to discuss this with a loving and trusted parent will be a real bonus. Don't tell them what they should do but help them to reach their own decision.

Throughout history Pisces has been assigned to the water lily, iris, violet, weeping willow and all trees that grow by the water. Growing these in the garden can be of benefit but if that is not possible, a picture on the bedroom or playroom wall would suffice.

Famous Pisceans

Rex Harrison
Frédéric Chopin
Harry Belafonte
Edward Kennedy
George Washington
Elizabeth Taylor
Michelangelo
Ben Lexcen
Percival Lowell
Michael Caine
Albert Einstein
Pierre Auguste Renoir
Eva Longoria
Christian Clemenson

Rihanna
Daniel Powter
James Blunt
Jon Bon Jovi
Carrie Underwood
Alan Rickman
Dr Seuss
Mickey Spillane
John Steinbeck
Victor Hugo
George Frideric Handel
Maurice Ravel
Rimsky-Korsakov

A little more on personality types

Carl Jung is credited as being the father of modern psychology but most people don't realise that Jung was also an astrologer. In fact, his system of personality types, upon which the most common personality tests used in business and schools are based—the Myers-Briggs, the Keirsey and the Eysenck—is related directly to the classification of personality types developed by the ancient Greeks and used by all astrologers. Table 1 shows the development over the past century to today's tests, based on ancient knowledge.

Jung was well versed in mythology and drew on the ancient archetypes in his work. An archetype is a word that describes a universal theme, such as Diana, the ancient Goddess of Love, or Hercules and his modern-day equivalent in the character Luke Skywalker from *Star Wars*. These same archetypes are also used in astrology. Psychology is not new; it dates back thousands of years. As long as humans have searched for order they have been trying to understand the 'psyche', an ancient Greek word that means the concept of the self, encompassing the modern ideas of soul, self and mind.

Jung also used the dual division of introvert/extrovert, creating eight possibilities in all when combining extrovert/introvert with the four elements. Introvert is categorised in astrology by a

Table 1 Personality types

Element	Astrology	Humor/Temperament (Hippocrates/Galen)	Jung	Myers-Briggs	Keirsey
Fire	Spirit	Choleric/hot	Intuition	NF (intuitive feeling)	Idealist
Earth	Physical	Melancholic/dry	Sensation	SJ (sensing judging)	Guardian
Air	Thought	Sanguine/moist	Thinking	SP (sensing perceiving)	Artisan
Water	Emotion	Phlegmatic/cold	Feeling	NT (intuitive thinking)	Rational

Table 2 Correlations between Jung and astrological terms

Jungian	Astrological
Intuition	Fire (Aries, Leo, Sagittarius)
Sensation	Earth (Capricorn, Taurus, Virgo)
Thinking	Air (Aquarius, Gemini, Libra)
Feeling	Water (Pisces, Cancer, Scorpio)
Extrovert	Most planets above the horizon
Introvert	Most planets below the horizon

Table 3 Major planetary cycles

Planet	First square	First opposition	Second square	First conjunction
Sun	3 months	6 months	9 months	1st Birthday
Mercury	8–16 weeks	5–7 months	8–10 months	11–13½ months
Venus	10 weeks–6 months	4½–8½ months	7–11 months	9½–13½ months
Mars	4–11 months	9–15 months	13–19 months	18–24 months
Jupiter	2 years 6 months–3 years 2 months	5 years 8 months–6 years 5 months	8 years 1 month–9 years 11 months	11 years 3 months–12 years
Saturn	6 years 5 months–8 years 1 month	14 years–16 years 1 month	20 years 11 months–22 years 9 months	28½–30 years

predominance of planets below the horizon at the time of birth, while extrovert has the majority above the horizon.

More on planetary cycles

The cycle of the sun is exactly one year, give or take six hours. The cycles of Mercury and Venus are on average one year, but vary. The effect of this is that some children will have all three of these cycles moving in synchronicity, creating regular 'leaps' in their development. Others will experience a wide divergence in the timing of the cycles and will tend to evolve at a slow and steady pace through the early stages of life. The order of the planetary experiences determines the individual makeup of each child's personality.

Table 3 shows the major developmental planetary cycles and the variance within which they occur. The variations are caused by a number of factors, including the elliptical nature of the planets' paths around the Sun and the time at which a child is born in the cycle. It is all relevant when mapping the evolution of the child and there are many variations that can occur: yet another reason why all children do not grow their teeth at exactly the same age, or crawl, walk and talk at exactly the same time.

Understanding your child's birth chart

Table 4 shows the glyphs for the planets, signs and the stronger aspects to help you follow your child's chart as you read *Star Parenting*.

Table 4 Understanding your child's birth chart

Sign	Glyph
Aries	♈
Taurus	♉
Gemini	♊
Cancer	♋
Leo	♌
Virgo	♍
Libra	♎
Scorpio	♏
Sagittarius	♐
Capricorn	♑
Aquarius	♒
Pisces	♓

Planet	Glyph
Sun	☉
Moon	☽
Mercury	☿
Venus	♀
Mars	♂
Jupiter	♃
Saturn	♄
Uranus	♅
Neptune	♆
Pluto	♇

Aspect	Glyph
Conjunction	☌
Opposition	☍
Square	□
Trine	△
Sextile	✳
Retrograde	℞

Glossary

Air signs Gemini, Libra and Aquarius.

Angles The angles of the chart are known as the midheaven (MC) and ascendant (rising sign). The MC is the point directly above at the time of birth and is considered to represent our aspirations in life. It is associated with career and status. The ascendant is the point of the ecliptic that is rising in the east at the moment of birth; it is the point that connects the heavens to the earth. In the horoscope it represents the self and the ability to impact on the world and how the world impacts on us. Angle also refers to aspects (see below).

Ascendant The degree of the zodiac rising on the eastern horizon at the time of birth.

Aspect An aspect is simply the angular separation (degrees) between any two objects or points. The ones that are the most important are the conjunction (in the same space 0 degrees), opposition (180 degrees), square (90 degrees) and trine (120 degrees). They carry energy between the planets/points but will either blend it smoothly or with difficulty depending on whether it is a 'hard', square or opposition, or 'soft', trine, aspect.

cardinal signs Cardinal refers to the beginning of the four quarter divisions of the year and zodiac. These signs are

Aries, Cancer, Libra and Capricorn and are considered to be the initiating, energetic, self-starters of the zodiac.

Earth signs Taurus, Virgo and Capricorn.

Elements Fire, Air, Earth and Water.

Fire signs Aries, Leo and Sagittarius.

Fixed signs These four signs—Taurus, Leo, Scorpio and Aquarius—are the middle of the four quarterly divisions and are considered to be stabilising, committed and unwavering.

House One of the twelve divisions of the horoscope. The houses symbolise the twelve sectors of action in the individual life. The most important of these are the angular houses first and seventh, as shown by the ascendant/descendant point, and the fourth and tenth, as shown by the midheaven position. This is known as the Cross of Matter and defines the individual, our heritage, how we relate to others and our aspirations.

Luminaries The Sun and the Moon are not planets and are referred to as luminaries, in that they illuminate, or give light.

Midheaven (MC or Medium Coeli) The point of culmination of the Sun. The highest point on the ecliptic where it intersects the meridian. The MC should not be confused with the zenith which is directly overhead on a line drawn through the observer from the centre of the earth. The MC lies on the ecliptic which is the path of the sun across the sky.

Mutable signs The mutable signs are the final third of each of the four quarter divisions and encompass the signs Gemini, Virgo, Sagittarius and Pisces. The mutable signs are considered to be fluid, changeable and impulsive.

Personal planets This is the term given to the Sun, the Moon, Mercury, Venus and Mars, as well as the ascendant (rising) and midheaven (MC). As these parts of the horoscope are the fastest moving they are 'personal' to the individual, not shared with larger groups. For example, in order to share an ascendant degree, two babies would need to be born within four minutes of each other in the same location.

Retrograde Having apparent westward ('backward', against the order of the signs) motion along the ecliptic, in an opposite direction from the usual or direct motion. All planets have a regular retrograde period, dependant on their individual cycle around the sun. The Sun and the Moon do not go retrograde.

Water signs Cancer, Scorpio and Pisces.

Zodiac A band approximately 16 degrees wide with the ecliptic in the centre. The Sun, the Moon and the planets travel essentially within the band of the zodiac. On earth this band is encompassed by the Tropic of Cancer in the north and the Tropic of Capricorn in the south, with the equator marking the centre (ecliptic).

Acknowledgements

Putting together a book involves many people, not just the one who writes the words. I thought it was a fairly simple process before I began but was soon to find out how wrong I was. To that end I want to thank Maggie Hamilton, my angel from Allen & Unwin, who had the vision to birth the Inspired Living imprint. It was also Maggie who in her wisdom approached me with the idea to write this book. *Star Parenting* had been a dream for a long time but Maggie made it a reality; thank you, Maggie. I must also thank Ros Burton from Adyar for bringing Maggie and me together, as well as Aziza Kuypers, Kathy Mossop and all of the wonderful staff at Allen & Unwin.

On a more personal note, I thank my partner Ed Tamplin whose perseverance and striving for excellence over many years has helped improve my writing style to the point where I could make *Star Parenting* happen. I love you, Ed. Of course my children have all contributed much to the experience I have drawn from when putting all of the information together; our children have much to teach us if we are willing to learn. Finally I wish to thank my youngest daughter Caitlin and granddaughter Olivia for their love and support and especially for putting up with my moods and panic attacks, and for being my sounding-board.